Tennessee Hollow to Michigan's Motor City

o———o

1942-1952

Tennessee Hollow to Michigan's Motor City

1942-1952

by
SALLY DUDNEY CARNEY

To my dear friend Barbara — ! Enjoy

Sally Carney

Saginaw, Michigan
2014

CONTENTS

PART ONE
*Gainesboro, Tennessee Childhood Transition to
Detroit, Michigan Childhood
1942-1948*

Chapter 1	Wilmore Hollow	11
Chapter 2	Preparations for Journey to Detroit	21
Chapter 3	Making Detroit Home	27
Chapter 4	New Church Ways	33
Chapter 5	New Friends, New Risks	39
Chapter 6	Beginning School in Detroit	43
Chapter 7	Uncertainty at Home	45
Chapter 8	The Piano Plan	49
Chapter 9	Piano Lessons	53
Chapter 10	A Family Changed	59
Chapter 11	From Duplex to Flat	63
Chapter 12	A New House, a New Sense of Self	67

PART TWO
*Detroit, Michigan Teenage Years
1949-1952*

Chapter 1	Arriving at Cass Technical High School	75
Chapter 2	Beginning Classes	79
Chapter 3	Insights	81
Chapter 4	From Confusion to Clarity by Graduation Time	85
	Epilogue	89

I was a child of the hills.
My resolve was cast
In their bedrock womb.
My imagination soared
Past their summit.

Sally Dudney Carney

PART ONE

*Gainesboro, Tennessee Childhood
Transition to
Detroit, Michigan Childhood
1942-1948*

CHAPTER ONE
Wilmore Hollow Childhood

A dim awareness of war enveloped my eight year old mind but what that war would mean for me and my family would take years to learn. The Second World War came when my family and I lived on Tennessee's Great Cumberland Plateau. Within that auspicious area were small communities named Gainesboro, Whitleyville, Free State and Stone. Pioneering ancestors had carved those communities into the foothills of the Cumberland Mountains, along the Cumberland River; they had been, for over a century, home to generations of my family.

In October 1942, Mama, Daddy, Sister and I called the Wilmore Hollow, near Whitleyville, Tennessee, our home. The Wilmore Hollow Place was a tenant farm owned by a man named Jonah. He was short in temper and height, wide in boasting and girth. He wriggled his neck up and out of his collar when he spoke, as if mimicking our Bantam Rooster. He was a banker, in comfortable financial circumstance, with a tenant farm for rent to anyone who would plow the rocky hillsides, pay rent to live in the house and earn part of the crops' profit. That is, if there was a profit. Daddy rented the house, plowed the rocky hillsides and accepted all Jonah's conditions.

Jonah assumed a man of little intelligence would accept his terms; he lacked the capacity to understand the desperate circumstances that could make a man in need accept them. Even though he profited from Daddy's hard and careful work, he showed him little respect. He was often heard telling men, who sat on feed sacks around the wood stove at Whitleyville's general store, that Daddy was smart enough to plow his land but not smart enough to own it.

Daddy was born with awe for all things growing. He marveled at soil's miraculous way of sprouting seeds. He often stopped, scooped a handful of soil, smelled it, felt its graininess between his fingers and broad thumb, then made subtle distinctions—waxy soil would be difficult for sprouting seeds, clay soil was all right for potatoes but not good for corn or tobacco. In those hills, at age thirty-eight with an eighth grade education and farming his only work experience, he found work scarce or not at all. Daddy needed the tenant farm work to support himself, Mama, Sister and me.

There were caves and springs near the hollow, places formed by geological events eons of time ago. A place called 'The Big Springs', was located just around the hill at Whitleyville. The springs captured my young imagination with their mysterious darkness and depth. Folklore said it was a bottomless spring. These many years later its name evokes, in me, feelings of intense wonder.

The narrow road we traveled into the hollow followed the gentle Jennings Creek; the road bore ruts the width of wood wagon wheels and when riding on that road, it looked as if it would end but the bending creek pointed its direction and the road continued along beside it. Dust from the dry ground rose under the mule's hooves and settled on Queen Anne's Lace heads, the mule's leather reins, and on my tongue. Most remarkably, it settled on my sense of smell; that mysterious storage place in my body where a myriad of identifiable smells are kept. My joy quickened at the first glimpse of our house. Deep green Cedars, rising gently up the hillside, were backdrop for the house's red-brown rusted tin roof.

The Wilmore Hollow place was a 314 acre farm, covering mostly rocky hillsides with projecting limestone ledges. There was little bottom land; level land, where water didn't run off the crops and was a flat terrain for easier plowing. Ubiquitous red clay, emblamatic to most of the state, was the soil that made up the Wilmore Hollow farm. Despite that soil's unfriendly make-up for corn and tobacco, they were the main crops grown in the hollow. The part of the hollow that was not plowed was treed with old Oak, Sycamore, Box Elder, Cedar and Pine; these trees had grown unobserved except for the wide open eyes of the hills and unrecorded but for the growth rings numbering their years. The sun made sparse patches on the ground when its rays could pierce the trees' Crow and Blackbird filled branches. The crows' cacophonous songs called from the trees and in flight. Rattlesnakes, Blacksnakes and Copperheads moved silently on darkened paths under a canopy of undisturbed growth. There were mysterious places on the densely tree shaded hill. Varying sizes of moss covered, flat sarcophagus shaped stones rested on the few level places among the trees. Clumps of Pine needles huddled protectively around the ancient stones. Mama told us the stones marked the graves of Cherokee Indians, who lived on this land years ago. We were always to be careful and respectful of the grave markers and never walk on them because a human body was buried in the ground beneath the stone. When we walked the hill to find our Christmas tree, we were to be especially careful not to drag our tree over the mossy stones.

The log farmhouse, a small smoke house and two barns were the four buildings on the farm. The log house had been covered long ago with wood clapboard, but the original logs could still be seen at certain places where the clapboards had fallen away. The smokehouse stood just outside the kitchen door and at a greater distance stood the barns. The house was shaped like the letter T; our kitchen and bedsitting room were the top of the T that pushed up against the rising hill. The tall line of the T was the front of the house, shaded on each side by a covered open porch. At the back, the house was staked to the ground by a stone chimney.

The kitchen was home to a cabinet with specified places for stored spices and flour. Spices sat on a narrow shelf at the top of the cabinet and were closed from view by a wood-slat door that rolled up and down like a window shade. I imagined the spice boxes waiting in frozen stillness for someone to find them, the way I waited when playing hide-and-seek at dusk. The flour sifter, hanging in its wooden shaft, was always covered with a dusting of flour from Mama's last batch of biscuits. The cast iron cookstove sat firmly in the middle of the kitchen, where its neck-like pipe reached to the ceiling. Mama rubbed and polished the stove's belly and curves to a soft black glow. Its surface was warm from the cooling firewood and leftover cornbread with crisp corners was often found in its oven.

The room with the fireplace served as the bedroom as well as a sitting room for the four of us. That room was furnished with a battery powered Philco radio, four chairs with split oak slat seats, two tables and two iron double beds. The beds were covered with heavy quilts Mama had sewn and quilted from saved cloth scraps. Light weight pink bedspreads covered the quilts and were the only pieces of bedding Mama had not sewn. Mama crocheted in her rare resting time and one of her crocheted scarves covered a square table we called a washstand. An Aladdin kerosene lamp sat on the crocheted table scarf. Against the opposite wall from the fireplace stood our library table. Daddy met a man, who wanted to trade the library table for his shot gun. I never knew the man or the time and place of their meeting but I know the table had taken Daddy's eye and he was willing to make the trade. We took particular pride in its fine-grained, polished wood top resting on bulging, reeded legs. We were accustomed to dark stained and deeply grained oak furniture, far different from the new table's wood. Shades of red from the fireplace fire and the bedspread's pink glow filled the room with the look of sunset and the excitement of visitors. We sat around the fireplace or the kitchen stove when company did visit. The year's inside time was spent in those two rooms. Summer found us on the porches.

The front room of the house, without a fireplace or stove, was used only in warm weather. There Mama hung damp clothes to dry or set up her quilting frames. A small room, no bigger than a large closet and not part of the greater house, was right outside the front door. It was a strange little room, having its only entry off the porch. During summer, Mama allowed Sister and me to use it for our playhouse. Daddy made two doll beds from scrap wood, and Mama gave us cloth to dress the beds and make them soft. We put our dolls on their new beds and ran from the house to play. On our return, we took a quick look at the dolls to find a Rhode Island Red hen sitting on one of our doll beds! When we entered the little room, the hen did not fly off the bed as we expected but stayed perfectly still. We quietly stooped for a closer look. Her shinning black, unblinking eyes starred straight ahead. Unsuspecting of her purpose on our doll bed, we continued stooping and staring. She was laying her egg on our doll bed! We witnessed the unforgettable sight of her ruffled red-black feathered body and her fresh egg on our doll's bed.

Upstairs, under the steeply pitched roof, was an unfinished space that housed only seldom used articles. The underside of the tin roof was ceiling to the never-finished room. Two sources of light entered upstairs: timid downstairs light that crawled through the stairway opening and a few stingy, uneven lines of outside light that came through cracks at the roof line. In bright daylight, the cracks of light were more blinding than illuminating. I remember Mama taking Sister and me upstairs where she found, among other stored items, a deep stiff cardboard box. She carefully opened the box to show us her wedding dress and shoes. The dress was made of brown georgette and the narrow heeled shoes were covered with snake skin and soft brown suede. She told us she had earned money, to buy the wedding clothes, by picking field peas. She told us the hot sun beat upon her head, making the rows of dried brown peas seem endless. She had bought the dress and shoes at Ben Baugh's Dry Goods store in Gainesboro; ready-made clothes were shipped up the Cumberland River by flatboat to Butler's Landing then carried by horse and wagon to the Gainesboro store. The flatboat goods had come from Nashville, Tennessee and Asheville, North Carolina. She and Daddy were married in November, she told us, when the field work was finished. We watched with expectant and curious eyes as Mama packed the ancient-seeming wedding garments back into the stiff box. We left the shadowed upstairs in the silent company of itself.

Before-daylight found Daddy going straight to the barn where our animals awaited his coming and their first feeding. On one of his return trips to the house, he stopped at the smokehouse where he climbed on a small wood ladder to reach a slab of bacon hanging from the smokehouse rafters. Pre-dawn light in the smokehouse made it difficult to distinguish shadow from object, yet he sliced the bacon by that light. Before climbing down, he saw on a toe sack leaned against the smokehouse wall, an almost imperceptible movement, like darkness turning to light. He carefully climbed down the ladder and stealthily circumvented the toe sack to reach for a nearby ax. Without having a clear view, instincts stored in his mind's rafters told him the shadow was a waking snake. In the darkened light, his ax came down on the snake's body a few inches from its head. As daylight overtook darkness he saw the snake he had killed was a poisonous Copperhead. The head, not completely severed, continued to strike; the tenuous piece of connecting skin prevented the head from striking him. He reached for the sliced bacon and took it into the kitchen where, to our wide-eyed and breathless faces, he told us of his early morning chance happening.

Mama's workday began in the kitchen. After breakfast, I watched cottage cheese curds tumble to the bottom of her pan when she drained off blue-white milk. She put pork fat, wood ashes and lye in a cast iron wash kettle over an open fire in the yard; it bubbled and boiled until it became soap. She poured the boiling mixture into pans where it hardened and at the right time she cut the solid piece into small cakes of creamy white soap. I also eagerly waited while she gathered scissors and newspapers to cut a dress pattern for me. Holding the newspaper to my body, she cut a perfectly fitting pattern. She knew where to sew the tiny darts that turned flour sacks and dress fabric into dresses. My days were filled with watching Mama make things and discovering things I too could make.

Peddler Ray's mules pulled his painted red wagon, with hinged foldup sides, into the hollow during the summer months. He raised the sides to show Mama new goods stacked on shelves and packed in boxes. Pulses of delight rushed through me when I smelled the new fabric and household objects in painted paper wrapping. Peddler Ray knew Mama liked new fabric, though she rarely bought any. He slowly unrolled a bolt of dress goods near my eager face. Mama had a way of telling nothing by her facial expressions but the peddler watched closely regardless of her expression. He knew she was conjuring up a new dress in her mind. When he did make a sale, he cut the fabric from the bolt and held the folded piece against an open drawer of colored thread, hoping Mama also needed it. Peddler Ray sold Mama ordinary goods that she sewed into extraordinary things.

We went to the store on Saturday. If we needed a few things, we went to the Whitleyville store. Daddy climbed on the mule, I climbed behind him, Mama behind me, and Sister behind Mama and we rode to the store. If we needed a twenty-five pound sack of flour or to have our corn ground into cornmeal at the gristmill, we climbed into the wagon hitched to our team of mules and rode on the bumpy road to the mouth of the hollow where it turned onto County Road #56. That road ran between Whitleyville and Gainesboro. When we heard Daddy call "Haw" to the mule team, we knew we would turn left on the road to Gainesboro. It was a bumpy ride for Sister and me in the bed of the wagon. Sister and I held on to the sides of the wagon, bouncing and giggling. However, giggling was partly excitement at the prospect of going to town. Mama sat up front on the driver's seat with Daddy where she folded a quilt to soften her ride.

Gainesboro was six miles from our house. We rode past Stone Community and the house where I was born. Mammy and Pappy Roberts, Mama's mother and father, still lived there.Their house was across the road from the Johnson Cemetery where many of our relatives were buried. The road continued on to the Cumberland River Bridge. As we started over the bridge, the sound under the wagon changed. A hollow sound came from under the mule's hooves and a whirring silence surrounded us; we were high over the Cumberland River. The floor of the bridge was made of wood and covered with much dust from the dirt and gravel road we'd just traveled. The dust, thick and soft, powdered the bridge's wood floor. Daddy looked down, from the rolling wagon crossing the bridge, and saw corn and tobacco fields below. He said it was rich, black soil, some of the richest bottom land in the county and the richest he had ever seen. The plow, he said, rarely hit a rock. When the empty, silent sound no longer whirred around us, we knew we were over the bridge and only minutes from Gainesboro. We traveled to Gainesboro, the county seat of Jackson County, roughly once a month.

Going to town meant seeing relatives and friends as well as buying things we needed. We saw farmers sitting on the low brick retaining wall that wrapped around three sides of the Jackson County Courthouse. The yellow brick court house and grounds, set in the middle of town, was called 'Town Square.' We saw stores, the Post Office and people going about their chores. Gainesboro was the only place where we saw many people together except at church.

Farmers, who sat on the retaining wall, wore starched white shirts under clean bib overalls. They had driven their mules and wagons into town early in the morning so they could find a seat on the low wall and look at others as they arrived. Predictably unsmiling but pleasant, the men said, "Hidy" as we rode past. Sometimes Mama, Sister and I climbed out of the wagon, before Daddy rode up the hill past the courthouse to hitch the mules. We visited our uncle and aunt who lived in a house at the edge of town. I liked getting out before we went up 'town hill' but also missed hearing the men greet us with "Hidy." Once when we rode past the men sitting on the courthouse wall, one of the men said to Daddy, "Raymond, I've been a 'wondering how an ugly thing like you could have them three pretty girls in your wagon." Daddy looked over at the man and only slightly hesitating replied, "Well, there's just some things a man's got to ponder." All in hearing distance chuckled in surprise at Daddy's answer.

We sometimes stopped at Uncle Jim's filling station. Uncle Jim, Daddy's uncle, owned Gainesboro's gas station. Unlike his brothers, he left farming many years ago and moved to Nebraska where he worked in oil fields. After being away years, he returned to Gainesboro and bought the town's gas station with his saved money. Daddy often talked of how well he had done by saving money and returning home to buy his filling station. When we stopped at the gas station, Uncle Jim gave Sister and me Co-Colas, the word he used for Coca-Cola. It was the only drink I had ever tasted that Mama had not made. I looked forward to holding the blue-green, curving glass bottle that pulled my lips down into it as I drank. The excitement of drinking Coca-Cola felt tingly, the way Coca-Cola made my tongue feel. Uncle Jim put the little pointed pleated caps under a bottle opener, popped them off and let them fall into a box before handing the bottles to us. Sometimes we took the caps out of the box and put them in our pockets to take home; we pretended they were small pie tins for our playhouse.

After drinking our Coca-Colas, we went up the embankment to Uncle Pete's and Aunt Bryanie's house. Their house had a living room without beds! A wool rug covered the floors and upholstered chairs were covered with Mohair, a sharp, picky material that picked the backs of our legs when we sat on the chairs. I loved the brown mohair chairs because they were upholstered. Mama told us upholstered meant they had springs in their seats and were covered with fabric. Aunt Bryanie allowed Sister and me to bounce on the chairs; she told us since we never got wild, the way some of our cousins did, we could bounce on the chairs while she talked to Mama. Sister and I bounced on the chairs because our Wilmore Hollow chairs were woven oak slats. There was nothing about them that bounced! Uncle Pete was the *Sally Ann* bread man. Mama said it was a good job and I always thought they were rich because they lived in town, had a wool rug and upholstered chairs. I was proud when I saw Uncle Pete drive through town in the *Sally Ann* Bread truck.

Ben Baugh's store was the next stop on our trip up town hill. The store was near the place where Daddy had hitched the mules and wagon. On our way, we walked past the Post Office. Sometimes Mama led us in a wide circle around the men standing outside the Post Office because, "You never can tell when one of them is going to spit tobacco juice and I don't intend to have us, in our freshly ironed dresses, ruined with tobacco juice before we even get the things we came for!" After we circled around the men, we got a look at the inside of the post office. I especially liked seeing the tiny doors on each mailbox. Each one had its own key and the brass doors were decorated in filigree patterns. I went there once with Mama's youngest sister, who was expecting a letter from a friend. She opened the tiny square, filigreed door with her own key to see if the expected letter was in the box. I could hardly wait to grow up and have a friend mail a letter to me.

Pictures of very ugly men lined the Post Office wall. I asked Mama why anybody would want their picture on the wall if it wasn't a good picture. She told me the men probably didn't want their pictures there but all those men had done very mean things and they were wanted by the law. I couldn't understand why any body would put pictures of ugly men, who had done mean things, on the Post Office wall. I thought to myself, I'd keep that a secret!

Having walked past the Post Office, we continued until we came to Ben Baugh's store. It was the store where Mama, years ago, had bought her wedding clothes. Ben Baugh's shirt sleeves were rolled just below his elbows, unlike the farmers who rolled theirs just above their elbows. Ben Baugh wore a starched white shirt and dark blue pants. He wore a tie and slicked his hair down with something shiny. A fancy wrist watch was strapped around one of his wrists. The store's familiar smell greeted us as we went through the door. The smell was part oil soaked floorboards and part new leather shoes in cardboard boxes. Shelves behind the counter were stacked with bolts of fabric and new shoes in their boxes. The best part of all was the smell of bolts of cotton dyed in colors that made me want to shout to anybody in hearing distance to come and look. Mine and Sister's 'Color House' colors, a game we played, never looked like the bolts of colored cotton at Ben Baughs! The reds and oranges were bold, the yellows shone and the greens and blues flowed like the creek. I could not take my eyes off them. Mama had to take my hand and lead me out of the store with my eyes still fixed on the bolts. Ben Baugh had a bolt of red Dotted Swiss that I hoped nobody would ever buy, because when I grew up and knew how to earn money, I wanted to buy the whole bolt just to hold, look at, and smell! Occasionally, Mama bought some cotton to make dresses for sister and me, but she never liked the red Dotted Swiss as much as I did. Sometimes, we just walked through the store to see what we had never seen and sometimes Mama just needed to think about a pair of shoes or a hat.

Daddy would have bought the big sack of flour and loaded it on the wagon by the time we came out of Ben Baugh's store. A smaller paper bag held coffee, tea and occasionally a tiny bag of chocolate drops. Our last stop in town was the hardware store for it was on the way out of town. There was always work to be done in the Wilmore Hollow requiring nails. Daddy would buy the nails while we looked at enamel coffee pots and pickle crocks.

Saturdays also found us readying ourselves for Sunday and church. We bathed in a round galvanized metal tub filled with water Mama had carried from the creek and heated to scalding on the cookstove, then cooled with cold creek water. Mama cooked most of Sunday's dinner on Saturday and readied our clothes by making sure they were clean and perfectly ironed.

Mama sewed in her rested times but those times seldom came. Hoeing the garden, shooting snakes and hawks, feeding chickens, making soap, stirring dirty clothes in the black iron wash kettle, hanging them to dry in the sun, ironing, planting gardens, canning food and cooking meals, filled Mama's days and spilled over into her nights. At times, I thought she would never again sew on the sewing machine where she stored sewing treasures in the darkly stained oak sewing machine drawers; spools of colored thread, lengths of lace and pearl buttons sewn on a piece of cardboard awaited her. I longed to see and touch those treasures when she opened the drawers. I wanted lace sewn around my collar, pearl buttons sewn down the front of my dress and all Mama's rested times sewn in my seams!

There was both good and bad to liking the dresses Mama sewed for me. The dresses that brought pleasure also brought pain. I often watched her rub the flatiron back and forth across dampened cloth to bring a dress to life from a crumpled roll. The iron, kept hot on the cookstove, brought out the fragrance of sundried cloth and white lye soap. Those powerful fragrances drew me to the dark room at the front of the house where Mama hung the ironing on a wire line to season out. I went to that room once and put on each dress she had ironed and hug on the line for dampness to dry. I stood for minutes enjoying the sensation before I removed one dress and put on the next, letting the one I took off drop to the floor. In the midst of my dress changing, Mama opened the door. After seeing the efforts of her ironing laying on the floor, without explanation she taught me there was more than one point of view to freshly ironed dresses. I suffered, in silence, Mama's spanking on my legs!

Days and years were filled with Daddy going to the hillside to plow or tame a mule. It was not an unusual sight, in 1940, to see Daddy knocked from his feet and dragged several yards before recovering his stance to walk in the direction of his choosing rather than that of the mule. Mule taming was an integral part of the ongoing ritual of farming. An aging or tired mule would need to be replaced by a younger one. One that would be waiting if the older one balked on a particularly hot day. Mules were known to stay with a farmer for as many as forty years, not an easily ended relationship after that many years of gentle partnership. A sharpened plow shear and a trusted mule were the main tools of Daddy's farming life.

Daddy returned to the house, after the morning plowing, to eat the noon meal Mama had cooked and would set before him; he had observed the overhead sun and remembered how early he had eaten breakfast. He walked from the fields to the back porch where he removed two full dippers of water from the water bucket and filled a white enameled washpan circled with red paint. He washed the dirt and sweat from his face and hands then methodically tossed the water onto the yard. He wiped the edge of the pan with his hand, leaned it up against the house on the porch bench, then dried his face and hands. He sat at the table and began the noontime prayer before a bite of food was eaten. He thanked God for his work and asked God to bless us and forgive our sins. At eight years, I had heard the preacher talk about sins, but had not been able to understand what our's were. After the noon meal and a short rest on the porch, Daddy returned to his mule and plow to take up the work that seemed endlessly repeated. This was my world of eight years. I neither dreamed of nor knew to want a different one.

CHAPTER TWO
Preparations for Journey to Detroit

News of the war was broadcast over our battery powered radio on a Sunday. Sundays were quiet in the hollow because work ceased. The normal Sunday quietness turned to complete silence after the war news. An interminable stillness settled over the hollow. The news came the way a thunder storm moves from the far edge of the sky, hides the sun with black clouds, and sends lightening streaks and thunder claps. This dark feeling, however, stayed far longer than a storm. A worrisome gloom settled over Mama's and Daddy's faces and told a story I could only partially know. What I could not know was the anxious turmoil within them. Smooth grey patches on the Sycamore tree where I had imagined shapes of objects and people, holding my attention for what seemed like hours, now held little interest.

Monday's work resumed but it still felt like a dark, quiet, Sunday. The day's talk took a new direction with unfamiliar words. Talk of crops and weather was exchanged for war talk. Talk of factories and jobs in a place called Detroit were often mentioned. For me, there was a missing link in the war talk. I could not equate war with factory jobs. My understanding of war was of people fighting, not jobs. The economic reality of making war equipment as a source of jobs was part of the grownup world I had not entered and did not yet understand.

At the dinner table, before the war, I often saw a far off gaze in Mama's eyes. I wondered what she was dreaming. Mama dreamed dreams and had ideas for her life other than farm work in the Wilmore Hollow. One night, when I was thought to be sleeping, I overheard Mama tell Daddy her dreams. She dreamed of several things: to live out on the front within seeing distance of a neighbor, have enough money to pay for our needs before the crops were harvested, have enough money for food even if the crops were poor and be able to buy things without charging them at Whitleyville's general store. Most of all, she wanted to live in a way where her days were not filled with more work than she could finish.

Daddy had no gaze at the dinner table but he too had dreams. He told Mama he hoped to own land and keep all the money when the crops were sold. An adult life of tenant farming had taught him there was no getting ahead, only going backward. I had not understood, that over time, these feelings and disappointments had silenced Mama and Daddy. I felt their silence. Joy was missing from their tense, tightly drawn faces. I pretended, at times, I would have said something that brought laughter and animation to Mama's and Daddy's bodies. I smiled at the pretend vision of Mama bending in laughter. It was only that, a pretend vision. It was not Mama.

Kibby Tayse, who lived beyond where the road ended in the hollow, always laughed when she visited us. A narrow path curved between the hills from our house to the place where Kibby lived and she often walked that path to visit us. I was happy when I saw her walking to our house for even the basket she carried seemed to be filled with laughter. Her apron covered, gathered skirt of tiny black and white checked gingham fell to her ankles showing only her black, puddle splashed, cracked leather shoes. She smiled and laughed when she saw me. Once she told me she had always wanted a little girl like me but the Good Lord had not given her one. She told me she watched my long curled hair bounce on my back when I ran. She told me that she pretended I was her little girl. Then, while laughing, she clapped her hands and said, "Lord-have-mercy, listen to old Kibby." I was wanting Mama to laugh like Kibby, and Kibby was wanting me to be her little girl. We were both pretenders.

Days passed and the hushed words that did get spoken were still about the war. All our families' lives seemed like a mobile where each family hung from a string and as the winds of war blew on one family, that family's circumstance changed and touched another family, leaving us all moving in different directions. The coming of the Second World War altered all our lives in unimaginable ways and brought an end to the quiet, predictable life I knew in the Wilmore Hollow.

Before I had become aware of the war, Mama and Daddy had anticipated it and had talked about the possibility of Detroit jobs for themselves. They had made the decision to leave the tenant farm, if the war-time-factory-jobs could be had, for it would be a way out of the back breaking farm work with too little pay. They hoped the factory jobs would help them realize their dream of owning Tennessee land, land they would move back to and live on when the war ended.

In seasons past, digging potatoes or chopping wood to warm the house would have been the daily plans. I would have eagerly awaited the wet days that forced Daddy inside where he and Mama would have talked. I would have looked forward to the time, just before lighting the kerosene lamp, when the fireplace glow softened the lines on their faces for a short time. The chores that were compelling before the war news now appeared to lack urgency. Our daily routine was shaken like the numbers in the cakewalk drawing.

My two uncles left home to become Marines, while our family was left in disbelief at the speed of their leaving. I could only imagine my own coming dislocation but theirs would be far greater than mine. Then, Daddy left for work in Detroit and again I was left in disbelief. On a cold day in October, I watched and heard Daddy leave the hollow, with his friend, in an automobile. They traveled to Cookeville where they would board a train for Nashville, Cincinnati, and finally Detroit. I watched the car leave the hollow and heard the wind rush behind it, leaving us without Daddy's protection. I was yet to learn his presence as well as his absence colored everything. I learned my happiness came not only from the sun hanging like a ripe peach between Cedars and the smell of earth after rain, but from Daddy's presence.

Life in the hollow was palpably different after Daddy left. Mama and I crawled in the furrows to dig the potatoes where she and Daddy had at an earlier time. She had loosened the large clumps of soil in the rows with a hoe but now her slender fingers clawed the loosened clay to reveal a potato, ready to be lifted from the furrow. Finishing every row, we put them in a toe sack that Mama dragged to the cellar. The crops had been harvested when Daddy left, and he no longer came from the hills to eat dinner but Mama made our dinner anyway. She set one place short of four. We bowed our heads in prayer but now Mama asked God to protect Daddy and bless his work, to keep us safe while he was away and to forgive our sins. We ate, but without the enthusiastic hardiness as when we ate with Daddy.

School was a place Sister and I went every week day. I have no recollection of its importance in my life other than a second hand way of experiencing its benefits; those benefits came from Sister's knowing how to read and reading aloud to me. I had not attended school long enough to arrive at that mysterious place where written symbols translate into objects and ideas that put a world in front of you; one you didn't know existed, one you learn about while you sit in your own chair in your own house. School, therefore, had taken a lesser role in my life after the war news because there was little time to think about anything but the war. Although now, we would be forced to think about leaving school too. I would not miss sitting on the long benches waiting my turn to go, with my reader, to my teacher's desk near the wood stove. She would listen to my reading, help me with difficult words and tell me to return to the bench to study those words. I wanted stories read to me!

I liked the story books and pencil-and-paper things about school but I dreaded recess. We took our collapsible aluminum drinking cups from the shelf at recess and carried them to the outdoor pump where the water gushed out, splashing my shoes and socks with the muddy water that had pooled around the pump. The strong smell of sulfur water erased any thirst I had. I did look forward to lunch time, not for the obvious reasons of wanting a break from school work but that I would see Daddy. He would be framed through the double, wide opened school doors as he approached the schoolhouse on mule back. He brought mine and Sister's lunch, packed in a small lard pail covered with an ironed napkin. Inside the pail we would find a fried chicken leg, hot cornbread muffins with ruffled edges, a dish of turnip greens, and sometimes a dish of blackberry cobbler. I couldn't imagine school without Daddy.

Mammy and Pappy Roberts' thought it best that Mama, Sister, and I move from the hollow and live in a small house just up the hill from them. That decision set me wondering what it would be like to live in yet another house. I remembered living in the Whitleyville house across the creek and up the hill near the larger part of the creek before we moved to the Wilmore Hollow. There, the creek rose often during heavy spring rains and came within inches of flooding our house. I remembered dark, one lamp lit rooms where during the night, my anxious aunts attended my mother's bleeding gums in the aftermath of having all her teeth pulled on the same day. I had felt safer in the Wilmore Hollow, for it was without the threat of flooding from the rising creek and the frightening memory of Mama's teeth pulling. To imagine living in yet another house, without Daddy, was a threatening prospect.

Four months after Daddy left for Detroit, one of his letters told us he had found a place for us to live. He would be telling us the exact time to come when he knew more details. Mama filled her days making all the changes needed to move. Much was unknown to her. Would we be in Detroit six months or two years, how much should we take, and what should be left behind? Daddy told her of the gas kitchen stove in the apartment, eliminating the need to move our round bellied cast iron cookstove. She stored it in Pappy Robert's grist mill. She also learned the apartment was already furnished with furniture. There would be little space for anything more. My aunt came and carried the library table and a small dresser to store in her house.

Mama held all the unknowns, about our move, inside herself as she helped pack our clothes, the slat bottomed chairs and two iron beds into a friend's truck. We all drove out of the hollow. We were on our way to Stone where we would move into the little house up the hill from Mammy and

Pappy Roberts. When the two iron beds were moved into the house, Mama, Sister and I slept there each night, waiting for Daddy to tell us the day to come to Detroit. On many of those nights, before falling asleep, I practiced holding the sights, sounds and smells of the hollow inside myself. I was like a weary rat searching for morsels of food; I wanted to remember all the chiseled facets of color and texture I knew in the hollow. I stored in my memory the color of light before daylight, the look of air at dawn, stones under creek water, soggy wet moss, the overpowering brightness of noon sun on dry rocks, cave openings and their shadowed insides, the uncertain depths of the Big Springs, insect wings and eyes among the blackberry bushes, the mixture of dry manure and dust, animal feces, grainy soil, corn and tomato seeds, the sticky wooly feel of tobacco leaves, thick cream after it was separated from the milk, thick blue-white buttermilk, lard, the animal's flesh and blood at hog killing time and of course the moss covered sarcophagus shaped stones among the hillside Pines. I wanted all the visions I could retain to cushion me in distant and unfamiliar places.

When Daddy's call came, in February, the blooming Jonquils promised spring in Tennessee. Mama, Sister and I boarded a train in Cookeville and traveled the same road Daddy had to Detroit. The train was crowded with uniformed military men and other families moving north. The jerking movements of the train straightened out and slowly turned to a faster and faster speed; it traveled at a speed I had never experienced. The uniformed men stood in the aisles with their arms, reaching above their heads, grasping hanging leather straps to steady themselves. Their bodies swayed and halted from the jagged motion of the moving train; their feet remained firmly planted around their bundles and bags. Children sat on their mothers' laps giving as many seats possible to other adults. Daylight turned to twilight, curiosity gave way to drowsiness and sleep came on by the repetitive, harsh, slippery sound of steel wheels racing against steel tracks. Sudden jerking motions occasionally disturbed my sleep but Mama's arms were always around me whenever I awoke even though she may have dosed. We traveled more than eighteen hours, broken by one stop in Cincinnati, Ohio before we arrived at Michigan Central Station in Detroit. During the trip, I had feared Daddy would be unable to find us in the crowded depot. I was unaware of gate numbers and train schedules. When I saw his face among all the others, I silently vowed I would never be separated from him again.

Detroit's freezing February air, rain mixed with snow, and concrete roads covered with ice and slush was not the promise of spring, yet that was the weather that greeted us as we left the train station in a car called a taxi cab. We rode, in the taxi cab, along East Jefferson Avenue. Detroit's sights loomed large through the taxi windows even though traffic threw slush and ice on our windows and blurred some sights. The wide, forceful Detroit River was near our right; the rippling eddies of Jennings Creek were no match for it. Detroit's brilliant electric lights shown all around us. Street lights, automobile headlights, advertising lights, and store lights became a continuous blurred line of colored light as we continued riding in the taxi. I had never seen a traffic light and imagined the round green and red lights to be something left over from Christmas. I had seen only one or two electric lights where we lived. The TVA source of electric power, established in 1933 had, after nine years, stretched electric wires only as far as Gainesboro. There, a light bulb high on a pole sparkled like a cluster of fallen stars in the black night. The hills and hollows still waited for electricity while Detroit's electric lights looked as if they would never dim or go out.

High above us, between East Jefferson and the Detroit River at East Grand Boulevard, stood a twenty-five foot high stove, made of oak but painted to look like a metal cast iron stove. The taxi driver told us that before Detroit was known for automobiles, it was known as the 'Stove Capitol of the World.' A tire, as large as the stove, also sat high above the moving traffic. We would soon learn the giant tire was part of the US Rubber Co., place of Daddy's new job! We turned left onto East Grand Boulevard and almost immediately slowed to a stop in front of a house numbered 177. Two of its many rooms would become our Detroit home.

CHAPTER THREE
Making Detroit Home

The new house was one that Mama's imaginings months ago, could not have envisioned. In front of us stood an elegant, three story house built for two families in the late nineteenth century. It was called a duplex. I would later learn a duplex was two houses, with identical floor plans, connected by a central dividing wall. Each side had a wide, open front porch under a roof supported by concrete columns. The front windows in each side of the house looked out on a broad front yard, sidewalk, and easement between the sidewalk and four lane boulevard. Similar houses stood across the street. Fifty years after its construction and unimagined at the time, the house now served a new kind of owner and occupant. It was now home to many renters of small apartments, cut within the original commodious space. Our's would be the first family with children.

We found our apartment at the rear of the house where we walked through a closed wood porch, painted gray, to get to our entry. Our apartment was half of the first floor of the original house. It included the back hallway, lavatory, stairways up and down, dinning room, kitchen and pantry. Small electric bulbs, hanging on cords from ten feet ceilings, lit our way into the rooms. The former dining room was now our bed-living room. The large pantry with glass doored cupboards quickly became the storage place for our Tennessee belongings. Mama had sent quilts, pillows, home canned food, and other small household goods by way of a few men, she knew, who were driving cars to Detroit. The items had found their way to the pantry shelves as Daddy had received them. Our tomatoes and green beans in icy blue-green Mason jars were stored on the shelves behind the glass doors, shelves originally made for china and crystal. Pillows and quilts were on the counter between the upper and lower cabinets. We knew our new apartment would be furnished with furniture, yet when I saw it, I wished for our library table and cast iron cook stove. The war catapulted us from hollow farm to unfamiliar city, from farm house to city house apartment. The war's reshuffling was especially apparent in this elegant house, with its scattered collection of renters in newly formed apartments.

Changes in our housing made for our greatest adjustment. Chores in our new surroundings were done in unfamiliar places and in unfamiliar ways. The laundry room, with an electric washing machine, was located in the basement. Another long chord, ending in a dimly lit bulb, extended from the ceiling, although it scarcely lit the dark, black-gray concrete space. Every renter in the house had laundry privileges and many times we waited for another renter to finish their laundry before we could begin ours. Water pipes, ending in something called faucets, poured water into concrete laundry tubs. Beyond the laundry room stood a herculean furnace that filled a deep, dark cavernous space; its ductwork formed wrapped, mummified arms reaching outwards and upwards from its body into the ceiling. A hill of coal, to feed its roaring belly, poured down behind it. The furnace heated the entire three floors of our side of the house. Mama no longer had to carry water from the creek to wash the clothes but there were other hardships. Carrying heavy baskets of wet clothes up and down basement stairs was something she had never done in the hollow.

Our kitchen was so unlike our hollow kitchen, at times it seemed Mama didn't know where to begin. She learned to tame the whipping, blue flames of the gas cook stove, as there was no longer need to carry firewood for our cast iron cook stove. There must have been times when she was stunned, as I was, at the new ways of accomplishing the same tasks.

Apartments with one bedroom and a kitchen had been partitioned off on the two floors above us. No apartment had its own bathroom; a bathroom with a white enameled bath tub was located on each of the upper two floors. These two bathrooms with tubs, served all renters on our side of the house. Each person thoroughly cleaned the bathroom and tub after using it, leaving it clean for the next person. Our apartment's small lavatory, with basin and toilet, was a luxury for us. Our Tennessee baths were taken in our metal tub in the kitchen and our toilet was outside.

A widow, named Mrs. Rich, owned the big house. Her entrepreneurial instincts had served her well since hundreds of families and single people were moving into the city daily, looking for jobs and housing. Her unmarried brother and sister, known to all the renters as Uncle Mac and Aunt Nellie, lived with her. They occupied the entire first floor and half of the second floor on the opposite side of the duplex. Uncle Mac and Aunt Nellie were shorter than anyone I knew. Their bright eyes shown through deeply wrinkled faces and they walked in short measured steps. Aunt Nellie's black shoes pushed up against her rayon-stockinged ankles making them look as if they spilled over her shoe tops. Uncle Mac's well worn tweed vest covered his rounded and protruding stomach. We learned they were born in Scotland, moved to Canada in their middle age, then to the United States. Their very attentive and quiet bull dog, in perfect proportion to the three of them, followed them wherever they walked.

Our days took on an altered routine after we were settled in our apartment. As in Tennessee, Daddy left the house early for his factory job while Mama, Sister and I stayed in the apartment. Mama did her work, cooking meals and doing laundry while Sister and I occupied ourselves in helping Mama and at times playing with paper dolls. Mama had packed my toy dishes, toy metal kitchen cabinet and two Tennessee Santa Claus dolls to be brought with us to Detroit. They were my only toys in our apartment. Sister had brought her doll, but appeared to be growing away from it. She was four years older than I and both in leaving Tennessee and arriving in Detroit, had played no leading role in my inner drama. In the apartment, we shared our studio-couch bed but were without that daily intimate connection of telling thoughts and ideas. We were together all the time, now that winter kept us inside.

In Mama's soft spoken yet stern and quiet way, she was trying to find her footing in the new city and house, and her attention was not on mine and Sister's need to be in school. When we left Tennessee, our school year would have ended in three weeks. Mama reasoned it would be unnecessary to enroll us in Detroit schools for such a short time. She was unaware that Detroit schools would be in session for another three and a half months, then two more months including summer vacation. Sister and I remained out of school and in the apartment for another five and a half months. I often wondered, in later years, if having no warm winter coats and boots influenced Mama's and Daddy's decision not to enroll us in school. Their riveted attention to work and adjusting to living in a place so unlike the place they left behind, left little attention paid to mine and Sister's need for school and companionship with children our age. During those turbulent times, it seemed no one noticed but the two of us.

There was one powerful exception to my lack of closeness with Sister. It was her willingness to read aloud to me. Our Tennessee teacher had sent with her, in our move to Detroit, a thick reading book filled with stories. I was reading words and simple stories but not the stories that carried you off the page to a place you never wanted to leave. Sister knew all the words. She read those stories aloud to me and many of them I asked her to read repeatedly! During the times she read to me, we were sewn together the way stories can sew you to somebody when other things can't.

When Sister was not reading to me, I had to find other ways to fill my time. My curiosity, about the multitude of new things to look at and new people to observe in the big house, was insatiable. Soon, I delighted in quiet observation of the house and its people from a position on the top step of our apartment's upstairs stairway. The door, ever so slightly ajar, shaded me from view to anyone on the second floor. I looked up and down the dimly lit hall and imagined the people living behind the closed doors. Those observations and imaginings gave me much to think about when I descended the stairs to our apartment. I once saw a white haired man, renter of a second floor bedroom only, leave his room carrying an armful of books. I wondered where he was going and if he liked stories as much as I liked them.

News of the boulevard house apartments spread quickly; new arrivals to the city hoped to live in the house. Many of the hopeful renters were family members or others known only by a familiar surname belonging to so-and-so's people over in such-and-such a Tennessee Landing, Bottom, Bluff or Hollow. If apartments were available, the new renters were welcomed by Mrs. Rich. She was learning to like the gentle, mild-mannered, southern people.

Mama taught Sister and me the way, she thought proper, to live in the big house: talk softly, always walk inside the house, wash our hands often, be pleasant when spoken to and never touch anything belonging to someone else! These teachings put us in good stead. Unknown to me was a rule that forbid children living in the house! Daddy's pleadings, through his friend who was also a friend of Mrs. Rich, had been fortunate for us. We were allowed to rent on probation that Sister and I would not disturb or be disruptive. It was a happy day for our family when Mrs. Rich told Daddy we could continue living there because Sister and I were causing no disturbance nor had we been disruptive!

I filled my days with listening and watching. I observed the way the Tennessee women, now factory workers, dressed. They hung their house dresses and cotton flour-sack smocks in the back of their closets along with their ribbed cotton stockings. They donned warm slacks, snow boots, and sweaters because Detroit winters were bitter cold and snow lay deep on the ground. They pulled hats, called turbans, on their heads. The turbans covered their hair and protected it from factory machinery. While new garments warmed their bodies, a new outlook warmed their feelings toward work. Overhearing their conversations in the laundry room, I never heard them complain about their factory work the way I had heard them complain about their farm work. I wondered if it was because they now worked inside, without 'baking their heads in the sun,' Mama always said, and knowing exactly when they could quit work. I remembered Mama telling Daddy that what she wanted most was having her days not filled with more work than she could ever finish. I knew too, these women received a paycheck every week. That was unimagined in Tennessee. Each day found them getting ready for their jobs long before it was time to report for work. They accepted each paycheck with visible pride and that prideful countenance identified them as upstanding, responsible and punctual workers.

Some workers worked in the daytime while others worked during the night. Some worked a shift called 'afternoons' where one worked part of the day and part of the night. I could never tell what time of day it was in the big house by the cooking smells. Renters cooked dinner whenever they came home from work and cooked breakfast before they left for work, regardless of what the clock said. Their work days were filled with some aspect of work before they began their factory work. They cooked meals to eat before leaving for work or packed lunches to take with them to work. Their Tennessee habit, staying busy and being productive, characterized all their behavior.

On days off work, the woman renters shampooed their hair, wound it on small aluminum curlers and wrapped their heads in pink or brown hairnets. They were then ready to began a frenzy of housecleaning and laundry. Upstairs-renters had to descend the basement stairway in our apartment to get to the one-bulb lit laundry room. Back from the basement laundry, they polished their furnished furniture with Old English Furniture Polish and made Sunday dinner preparations as well as preparations for their coming week's work.

The men shopped for the family's food at Hardy Hatcher's grocery store on the corner of Lafayette and Helen. Hardy Hatcher was also a Tennessean but unlike most, he bought a small grocery store where he now gladly took the factory-earned money in exchange for the food items the renters could no longer grow and can for themselves.

In time, I was invited to go to Mrs. Rich's side of the house and have tea with her, Uncle Mac and Aunt Nellie. It may have been her way of getting to know the child she deemed extraordinarily interested in the big house. Mama allowed the visit. I walked up stairs, through two very thick doors, I would later learn were 'fire doors,' to their upstairs hall then descended their front stairs to the main floor. A living room, larger than any I had ever seen, lay at the bottom of their front stairs. The beauty of their furnishings was astounding. A grand piano stood near the front windows facing East Grand Boulevard. Chairs, couches, tables and lamps, I later learned were Victorian furniture pieces, were placed in pleasing arrangements around the room.

Mrs. Rich ask me to follow her to the kitchen where we would have our tea. Aunt Nellie stored her tea cake on a shelf behind their pantry's glass doors. The same glass doored cupboards as in our apartment where we stored home-canned food. Uncle Mac sat at the kitchen table with me while Mrs. Rich and Aunt Nellie prepared tea. Before my tea was served, I was asked if I would like milk with it. My only experience with tea was drinking iced tea in Tennessee and I could not imagine iced tea with milk. I declined, only to see each of them pour milk into their cups of hot tea. I drank mine, without milk, thinking it was the best and first hot tea I had ever tasted. A slice of Aunt Nellie's tea cake helped inform my opinion! Mrs. Rich, Uncle Mac, and Aunt Nellie's complete acceptance of me gave me a grown-up feeling.

CHAPTER FOUR
New Church Ways

Our primary social contact, both in Tennessee and Detroit, was church. The Detroit group of Tennessee people set about recreating the church community they left behind. There was no evidence they entertained the idea of fitting into an existing group. Tennessee's square, white frame church buildings, with hills rolling and dipping behind them, could never be duplicated in Detroit but they insisted on the same order and manner of worship they followed in Tennessee. The center of our service was communion, the Lord's Supper. It was served every Sunday morning and again on Sunday evening for those unable to attend Sunday morning worship.

We had been in Detroit only a few months, when Daddy along with some other newly arrived-to-Detroit Church of Christ members, walked to the Church of the Messiah located on the corner of East Grand Boulevard and Lafayette. They inquired if there was any unused room in their building and would they consider renting to our small congregation. The Church of the Missiah, at 231 East Grand Boulevard, was one half block from our apartment. The proximity of that particular church building, to the boulevard house at 177, was essential. All who would go to church there would be walking, for no one owned an automobile. To the joy and thankfulness of Daddy's group, the Church of the Messiah people agreed to rent their basement room.

The 1875 Gothic building, was imposing in design and scale. I felt as if I was entering a storybook picture when I walked through its low clipped shrubs and looked up at the gray stone walls and stained glass windows. Carefully clipped grass formed neat edges along the walkway leading to the heavy entry door. Inside, dimly lit intricate wrought iron light fixtures cast exaggerated shadows along curved walls. That brief glimpse inside their sanctuary was all I saw before we descended the basement stairs to the rented room where our services would be held. Daddy's group immediately set about fitting the basement room with individual chairs, replacing Tennessee's long cushionless wood pews. A table, for serving communion, was placed at the front and center of the room.

In Tennessee, women in the church prepared white, unleavened communion bread. They scored it into tiny squares where it was to be broken. Home made grape juice was served in a tall silver colored chalice passed from one person to another. In Detroit, Daddy was told unleavened bread for communion could be bought at Detroit's Eastern Market. He and I rode to the market, on the Gratiot streetcar, and bought Matzo bread in a red and blue package. The dry and slightly browned Matzo wafers were laid on our communion plate and the chalice was replaced with a tray of tiny clear glass individual cups, each holding a sip of Welch's store-bought grape juice.

I sat behind men worshipers whose necks were deeply lined, tanned and wrinkled from years of field work in drying sun. After months of factory work, the hide qualities of their skin began to visibly soften. Their starched shirts, buttoned tightly at the neck, held a cushion of air between the shirts and their bodies. After a short time into worship the men relaxed, their breathing slowed and they settled into their chairs while their starched white shirts remained a distance away from their bodies. At times, I thought of the Church of the Messiah worshiping upstairs and the Church of Christ worshiping downstairs and I wondered if God saw the floor in between.

A disappointing difference for me, between Detroit and Tennessee worship, was the manner of baptism. When a person was baptized in Tennessee, the entire congregation slowly walked on moving, crunching gravel to the creek's edge directly behind the church building. There, to the soft and quiet singing of the congregation, the repentant person was lowered, by the preacher, into the water until they were completely immersed, then raised from the creek water as a new member of Christ's body of believers. In Detroit, there was no crunching gravel, nor creek. In a few existing Church of Christ buildings, at a great distance from our house, a small concrete pool was built at the front of the auditorium; there you could see the person being lowered into the water and then brought out of the water but the water could not be seen. A mural depicting hills, sky, a few clouds, and a distant body of water was eventually painted on the wall behind the concrete baptismal pool.

Mama's and Daddy's church and family teachings, their physical circumstances and Tennessee landscape had demanded all their strength. On Sundays, when factory workclothes were exchanged for church clothes, they reverently sang;

Work for the night is coming,
Work through the sunny noon;
Fill brightest hours with labor,
Rest comes sure and soon.
Give every flying minute,
Something to keep in store;
Work for the night is coming
When man works no more.

Sundays vitalized Mondays. Stamina had been needed to coax growth from shallow soil on rocky hillsides and stamina was needed now to get top production from factory machinery. They resolved to go beyond what was required.

On Mondays, I resumed my observations and contrasted my ever-present vision of the hollow with the activities and people I saw in our new house. Our Tennessee milk pans, with rock-weighted lids, sat on flat limestone rocks in the cold, gurgling water of Jennings Creek. Our milk in Detroit was kept cold by blocks of ice delivered, by an ice man, to each apartment ice box. The ice man's fifty pound block of ice was held by curved, sharp clamps attached to a heavy leather strap that rode over his shoulder as he climbed our back stairs. I remembered looking down from the barnyard fence and seeing the taunt leather rein riding over Daddy's shoulder as he put the mule through certain paces. The smell of cooking bacon brought back the vision of Daddy, silently going each morning before daylight, to slice bacon for our breakfast from a slab hanging in the smokehouse. Now bacon was bought at Hardy Hatcher's store and came sealed in a flat cardboard package with a small, clear window showing only the lean part of the meat. I carefully listened to the speech of renters who were natives to Detroit. The difference in their speech and the speech I was accustomed to was not only pronunciation, there was an absence of rhythm. I remembered the flowing, heightening, and sometimes billowing speech of Kibby Tayse. It moved in pleasing, spiraling, sounds and peaked as it splashed on my ears. That sound too was recorded and stored in that guarded place within me.

I silently began to walk through the second and third floor hallways of the house, where I got a closer view of its unfamiliar features. When I looked closely at the steel doors separating the two side of the house, I could see their thickness was the width of my arm's length. They were opened and secured to the wall by heavy chains. They were on both the second and third floors. Mrs. Rich passed me in the hall as I was looking at the massive doors and told me they were called 'Fire Doors'. The name conjured up yet another new and worrisome image.

After three months, Mrs. Rich observed my curiosity and knowing there was little to view from our rear-of-the-house-apartment, invited me to come through the second floor fire doors to her adjacent rooms. The entire first floor and the front half of the second floor had remained the private rooms for her, Uncle Mac and Aunt Nellie. We walked to her bedroom at the front of the house where the door was opened wide. I immediately felt the difference between a home with elegant furniture and a rented apartment with furnished furniture. Her bedroom was for sleeping only and all the furniture was matching pieces. Three large windows looked out on the tops of rising Elm trees that lined the boulevard. A narrow seat was built underneath the window. I kneeled on the bedroom window seat's soft cushion to look down on the broad street below. Moving automobiles, people walking past the house and children in groups of two and three roller skating, riding bikes and skipping rope were all below me. There was enough to gaze on for hours. Mrs. Rich did not hurry me.

My observations became a script for my paper doll play back in our apartment. Playing with paper dolls was my most satisfying play during those days without school. Sister and I fabricated an elaborate cardboard house. It's many rooms were decorated in the manner we wished our rooms to be. We used all the scraps of paper and fabric we could find and cut paper dolls from any paper picture of people we came across. I remember a Sear's Catalog that had holes in almost every page, holes made by our cutting a picture of a person or object from its pages. We made wardrobes for each doll by carefully drawing the doll's outline then drawing clothing over the outline. We designed and colored the clothes using crayons, pencils and pens. We secured the clothes to the paper doll by carefully drawing tabs that folded over the paper doll body. Those props provided hours and weeks of play. The cardboard house became the stage where I practiced speaking words the way I had heard them spoken by Detroit natives. I had a worrisome fear of being ridiculed for my southern way of speaking, and those playtimes provided complete freedom from that fear of teasing. Pretending held a ripeness for learning. I had heard Mama and Daddy speak of some southerners who were trying to get above their raising by speaking like the Northern people. I wanted to speak like others I had heard in the North, and had never thought about 'getting above my raising.' Our paper dolls spoke the way Detroit natives spoke.

One day ended and another began while I continued observing the house, its people and the seasons. Winter had seemed endless. The hills were never far from my thoughts. In Tennessee, I watched the sun move over the hollow and saw the hills cast tall shadows and within a few minutes, what seemed bright and clearly defined quickly changed to gray with blurred outlines. Gullies, no more than low places in the earth, became deep recesses without seeable bottoms. Many times, in Detroit, I felt like I was on the shadowed side of the hill. Inside me, much was gray and of uncertain depth. When Detroit's spring air came, it warmed my skin but not my deeper self.

Past springs would have found me sitting on the barn fence, waiting for ideas to come rushing into my head the way storms rushed in when Mama's wash was hung on the line. Ideas for discovering, and experimenting with found objects would have filled my mind. I would have jumped from the fence and rushed to undertake those ideas just the way Mama rushed to gather her wash before the storm. I made a skirt by pinning large Box Elder tree leaves together with thorns. After seeing the chameleon change its colors according to its resting place, I imagined sewing thread that would change colors to match each part of the fabric as it was sewn through it. I never tired of looking at the creek. The stone's colors were brilliant and I could find pebbles and pieces of moss the size I needed to make whatever I imagined. The hollow was my playground and nature provided plentiful toys. Birdsongs, heard high in the trees, accompanied all my creating journeys.

Making Color Houses in the hollow, was the play I missed most. Sister and I spent hours using a small rock to crush blossoms, leaves, grasses, insects, and berries on a flat piece of limestone. We scraped the substance into glass canning jars, filled the jars with creek water, screwed on a lid and shook them until surprisingly beautiful liquid color appeared. We set the jars, filled with colored water, in the sun or sometimes shade until they deepened and intensified. We didn't use the colors in any special way, we simply delighted in their mystery. Blue, green, orange, red, yellow and shades in between filled our jars and filled our minds. Early mornings melted into the heat of noon while we were at work with our colors. We were unaware of time passing. Summers came and went and we never tired of our color experiments. Wherever we set a jar of color among the trees, that place became the color's house. We visited each Color House with glee.

Not knowing what to expect when the seasons changed in Detroit, I was sure Spring was far away. There were fewer signs telling me Winter was fading and Spring was arriving. I saw small buds on some scrappy growth around the house and I heard spring faintly in the birdsongs but there was no rushing creek water and the smell of earth was gone! However, on a quiet warm morning, I walked from our apartment through the closed porch to the back steps and sat down. I heard again the bird's Spring songs, and looked up toward their flight. My eyes and nose were caught at the same moment by the sight and smell of purple buds. The unfurling blossoms covered the bushes I had thought were scrappy growth! The perfume and beauty of their color stilled me. Lilacs had blossomed overnight! These new Detroit fragrances called me, like a spring morning had called in the hollow. The fragrance of the Detroit lilacs curled into my nose and stayed in the same place as the smell of hollow dust on the Queen Ann's Lace heads.

I discovered that summer was easy to know in Detroit, though not through a smell or sound but a sight. Everybody got into their car and drove to Belle Isle. Belle Isle was an island in the Detroit River, connected to our side of the river by a bridge that was in walking distance of our apartment. At the intersection of East Jefferson and East Grand Boulevard, the Belle Isle Bridge began its span across the Detroit River to Belle Isle. A tunnel also ran under East Jefferson to the bridge. We walked from our apartment across East Jefferson and across the bridge to the island. People spread blankets on the ground for picnics, rode rented bicycles and paddled around canals in rented canoes. In the middle of a large open space was a great flowing fountain, designed by Cass Gilbert, who designed Detroit's Main Public library near the Art Institute. When dusk came, changing colored electric lights were turned on at the source of the rising water, making the water look as if it too changed colors. Forceful tunnels of water soared high through wide open mouths of grotesque faces, sculpted in concrete around the fountain. The changing colored lights and beautifully flowing fountain announced the arrival of summer in Detroit.

There had been endless possibilities for play in the hollow and there seemed few in Detroit. I needed money to buy playthings, if I was to join the children I watched from Mrs. Rich's upstairs bedroom window. I saw children skate on steel roller skates on the sidewalks and some rode bicycles. I had neither. I knew bicycles could be rented on Belle Isle but I had no rental money. I dared not ask Mama and Daddy for playthings. Their aim was to save enough money to return to Tennessee and buy land. I had heard them say many times that they were not spending money on trifling things, and I was sure the playthings I wanted would be thought of as trifling. I began to think how I might earn money, for I longed to join the children in play.

Later that very day, Mrs. O'Leary, one of the Detroit renters of an upstairs apartment, knocked on our door. Mama answered the door but it was not Mama she wanted. She told Mama that since she and her husband had been working much overtime, she had gotten behind with her ironing, especially handkerchiefs. She wondered, since I wasn't in school, if I might help iron the handkerchiefs and a few other flat pieces. She said she would pay me! I had been listening to every word she said. Mama turned to me and asked me what I thought. I began to tell Mrs. O'Leary how I had watched Mama iron and that I too could do a good job. Mrs. O'Leary smiled and said she had never doubted that in the least, that was the reason she was asking me! It was as if my thoughts of earning money for skates had been overheard!

CHAPTER FIVE
New Friends, New Risks

I had observed children playing outside our house through Mrs. Rich's upstairs bedroom window. Sometimes a few girls, who looked to be my age, clustered on the sidewalk in front of the big house. I longed to join them, but to do so was a risk. I was painfully aware of the differences in our speech and my lack of skates and a bicycle. One afternoon, after summoning courage from my speech rehearsals with the paper dolls and the prospect of having money to buy roller skates, I walked outside to the group of girls. I consciously left off the final syllable of 'Hidy', the Tennessee greeting, and said,"Hi."

One of the girls I met, named Sylvia, liked talking as much as I liked listening. I liked saying her name over and over to myself. I had never known anyone named Sylvia. It whistled and curled on my tongue and rolled off my lower lip. She invited me to play with her at her house. She asked if I liked playing with paper dolls, and if I did, I was to bring them along to her house. I told her I was sure it would be all right with my mother but I would need to go back inside the house to ask her, also to get my paper dolls. My excitement over the prospect of playing with a new friend could not be hidden from Mama.

Mama had strict rules that helped keep herself and me on the right track. She was silent when I told her of meeting a friend. She listened, while I talked about the girls not laughing at the way I spoke, about Sylvia asking if I liked paper dolls and if I could play at her house only three houses from our house! Mama spoke softly but sternly. Yes, I could go, but I was to look closely to see if it was the right kind of house. I would know, she said, if it was clean. She also said I was to listen to my friend's mama to hear if she used any ugly words. If she did, I would know it was not a fit place for me and I was to come right home! I thanked and hugged Mama and got my favorite paper dolls.

I had often walked by the creek in the hollow and seeing a rock, turn it over with my toes. Sometimes, a white and blinded insect scrambled to its familiar darkness, like tender exposed roots curl from the sun. Just then, I felt a particular closeness to the plight of all life kept in the darkness. Possibilities of exciting adventures had formed in my mind when I looked from Mrs. Rich's bedroom window and my darkened lookout on the top step of the stairway; now, possibilities were getting close to reality. The heat of reality made me want to scramble, with my vulnerability, back into the darkness yet at the same time, I had a great desire to be vulnerable. I ran from my house to Sylvia's house. We wasted no time in dressing our paper dolls and sending them to imaginary places acting in imaginary ways: church, a wedding, a moving picture show, out for dinner and to school. Some of the places I knew about, some I did not. I listened carefully to the unfamiliar places, wanting to know every detail. Hearing about school was what I liked most. It had been almost five months since I'd smelled the musty paper and waxy crayons of the hollow school. I thought of its windows, dressed in dark green frayed shades pulled half way down, yet through those windows the road and meandering creek were reassuring and alive. I listened to my new friend, trying to imagine the Detroit schools, hoping she would tell me more.

Sylvia described school but her descriptions were like a stuffed Christmas stocking; I could see the shape of the things, but details were missing. She told me about homerooms, a home economics room holding electric sewing machines and electric stoves, an auditorium, crossing guards and janitors who filled ink wells. I learned about writing pens with pen points dipped into the blackest ink poured into little glass inkwells set in a cut out circle in our desks; it was poured there each morning by a janitor, carrying a long, thin spouted watering can filled with ink. She told me about music classes with a piano in each room and art classes with cupboards lining the walls filled with colored paper, paint, drawing pencils, crayons, scissors, charcoal and art gum erasers for each student! She told me about the gymnasium, where a rope the thickness of our leg, hung from the ceiling and ended in a knot the size of our heads. Children climbed the rope as far as they were able, then climbed down where their feet were stopped at the knot and they could jump to the floor. There would be fire drills; a practice where we slid down a curved metal tunnel that descended from the second floor. The fire drill practice would lead us to safety in case of fire. She described the library where shelves, filled with books, lined its walls. There, a librarian read stories aloud to each class and children could borrow books to take home and read. I wanted to hear every thought and word Sylvia knew about school! She told me I could see for myself, come September. My new school's name was Field Elementary School.

Mine and Sylvia's friendship was like Mama's crochet hook and thread; we were knotted and looped together in an intricate pattern. Sylvia's last name was Webb. I liked the sound of Webb as much as I did the sound of Sylvia. On a sunny morning in Tennessee, I had seen the spider's delicate, night time work stretched across the barnyard fence. The overnight dew hung on the web like a string of glass beads. I thought of mine and Sylvia's friendship as that kind of web, sparkling. Her house had not been dirty and I had not heard any ugly words! My insatiable longing for friendship was beginning to be satisfied.

Soon after Daddy knew I was saving Mrs. O'Leary's ironing money, to buy a pair of roller skates, he came from work and handed me a heavy box. Inside was a pair of grey steel, oily looking roller skates with ankle straps of the brightest red leather I had ever seen. A key, needed for opening the washers on the bottom allowing them to extend to fit my shoes, came with the skates. Daddy tied the key on a long piece of heavy twine and told me to hang it around my neck because I would have to put my skates on and off by myself when he wasn't at home. He also told me he was proud that I had wanted to earn the money for the skates. He told me it took a whole lot of denying ourselves some little things if we ever wanted to get some big things. I knew what Daddy's big things were and I was happy he wanted me to have the skates before I had earned all the money. I gave him the money I had saved and we thanked each other. With my stack of paper dolls and the new skates, Sylvia and I played together every hour our mothers would permit.

Summer moved quickly with the roller skates. We skated up and down the sidewalks in front of the boulevard house and in the parking lot of the Christian Science Church located between our apartment and Sylvia's house. We skated in the mornings and in the afternoons. Within a few weeks, after many skinned knees, I gained a sense of balance. The buzzing sensation in my feet, after I took off my skates, became a favored feeling. It was second only to the excitement of putting them on, tightening the thick red leather strap and skating to Sylvia's house.

I discovered the best way to find another friend was through Sylvia. She introduced me to her friend, Gloria Wood. Her's was a name I took to as much as I took to Sylvia Webb. I thought I had sung songs in church about Gloria, and I was acquainted with wood. Gloria asked if I liked music. Of course, I liked music! We had cake walks in Tennessee and there was nothing l liked more than walking on the Free State School stage to the rhythm of music. Some of the men in our community played guitars and fiddles; Mama and Daddy were always pleased when we were going to have music at the cakewalks. However, I was to learn Gloria did not mean the kind of music

I had experienced. This second new friend opened an unexpected and glorious possibility for me.

Gloria studied piano; her's was a black grand piano with stacks of yellow music books resting on its cover. Music and books were stacked on the dining room table and by every chair and lamp I saw in her house. Gloria's family was friendly and kind to me. They were interested in my name and how long I had lived in the boulevard house and where I had gone to school. They listened attentively to all I told them; Daddy had gotten a factory job in Detroit and wrote to us in Tennessee that he had found a place for us to live and we too could move to Detroit. I told them about Mama not knowing the new school ways in Detroit therefore I had not gone to Detroit schools yet. After we had a visit, Gloria asked if I would like to hear her play the piano.

I had never heard anyone play the piano the way Gloria played. It was not only how well she played, it was the music itself. The children I had heard, 'banged' on the piano, as Mama would say. Gloria set a music book in front of her and began to play. She looked intently at each page, turning it carefully and rarely taking her eyes off it to look at the piano keys and her hands. She followed the notes as closely as Sister followed the words in the story books she read to me. Gloria was nine years old and had studied piano for five years. She practiced at least one hour each day and two or three hours on many days. She told me she loved playing the piano and loved her piano teacher. Her music awakened a sleeping place in me; a place I did not know existed until I heard Gloria play but I knew then, the yearning for it had been moving within me for a very long time.

CHAPTER SIX
Beginning School in Detroit

I walked with my two friends to Field Elementary School on the first day of school. I possessed new found confidence from hours of speaking practice. I was filled with high expectations from all I had heard about school and I was not disappointed! I was given a red paper notebook and on its cover was a pen and ink drawing of the Detroit skyline, superimposed with bold black letters **DETROIT PUBLIC SCHOOLS**. My teacher printed my name underneath those words and punctured the skyline picture with the tip of my writing pen holder, connecting it to my notebook. Every day my writing notebook was collected and returned to the storage cupboard. I eagerly waited for the next day when the 'notebook captain' connected my name to me and laid my notebook on my desk. This surely was evidence that I had a place here!

Sylvia's school descriptions, during the summer past, revealed themselves daily. Although Sylvia had told me about the building, its rooms and their equipment, I was to discover the school's people! They offered the Detroit welcome I had yearned for. The structure of each day was marked by variety in tasks and people. Each classroom had its own teacher, unlike my Tennessee classroom where a single teacher presided all day over eight grades. Each teacher's attitude toward me was caring, private and interested. A loud electric bell announced each class change, bringing with it a new set of experiences.

Vocal music class had its own teacher, piano, and shelves holding many song books; there was a book for each student. The blue Silver Burdett Company song book became my favorite. After a few weeks, I turned to *The Erie Canal*, when we were asked for titles we liked. I sang with gusto, "I've got a mule, her name is Sal, fifteen miles on the Erie Canal! She's a good ol' worker and a good ol' pal." Reinforcing smiles came my way while I sang.

My greatest fear had been my southern speech but somehow my speech became my greatest strength. I was asked to read aloud, take part in a play, and be the announcer for a school program. There were no sideward glances when I spoke. It never mattered to the teachers that I was from the South and didn't know all the ways like the other children, nor did it seem to matter to the other children.

Burning anticipation characterized the beginning of each day. Special trips and events were planned. A trip to the Detroit Institute of Art found me bending my neck backward to gaze high overhead at paintings by Diego Rivera. His paintings surrounded me. The painted workers were far larger than life and seemed to become even larger as I looked the distance above me. Their flexed muscles were repeated in scenes around the room, their bodies integral to the machinery; they were moving, expanding, producing even as they were stilled in the fresco. Up there and all around me, were paintings of workers like Daddy working the way he worked; the workers were immortalized through this industrial city's painting. It made me want to celebrate their worth. I felt recognized! On another trip, to the Masonic Temple Auditorium, lights dimmed and as my eyes adjusted to the bright stage lights. Karl Krueger entered the stage and conducted the Detroit Symphony Orchestra in music that filled the auditorium and my longing. I had never before seen or heard a symphony orchestra. Its array of musical instruments stunned me. Its music was Gloria's piano music and its lure was as profound as when I had first heard her play.

Teachers included our mothers in our learning. We demonstrated what we had learned by giving a luncheon for them. I sewed an apron in home economics class and wore it when we cooked and served white sauce with peas over toast. Mama came, dressed in her Sunday dress, and ate the sauced toast as if it tasted as good as her Angel Food cake. My teacher asked me if she could call my mother, to let her know of my need for extra help in long division. With patient teaching, after school, long division became my favorite mathematical process. I delighted in the long and sideward-moving problems. I made them as neat as Mama's bias seams. Even if something puzzled me, I felt there was nothing I couldn't learn with help.

CHAPTER SEVEN
Continued Uncertainty at Home

My attachment to school soaked up all my time and thought. While thinking only about myself, I had not been listening to Mama's and Daddy's daily talk the way I had before school started, and not observed that some of their old worries were settling in again. I was unsure how their days were beginning yet I felt they were not beginning as brightly as mine. Daddy worried about the prospect of being without work. It frightened him in a way that was difficult for me to understand. I thought, now that he had a job, there was nothing more to worry about. For Daddy, there was always something to worry about and the present worry was the threat of being laid off. At the time, he was home from work for a few days while the factory made 'change overs'. His inexperience with that routine and his natural inclination to worry, made him fear they might never call him back to work.

I often took naps on the quilts Mama laid on the counter tops in the pantry. During one of those naps, I was awakened by Daddy telling Mama that he was going to leave Detroit.

"I'm not going to stay here and starve without work, I'm going to go back home."

"What are you going to do there but starve? Are you going to feel any different starving in Tennessee than you would in Detroit?"

"I'll be near Pappy and I can find something to do."

"You were near Pappy before we came here and you couldn't find anything to do, what's going to be different now?"

"I don't know, I'm just not going to stay here and starve on the street."

"Well, it doesn't make any difference to me where you starve, but for me, if I'm going to starve, I'd rather starve here than there. I've grubbed in the dirt as long as I'm going to. There isn't anybody down there that's ever going to make anything out of themselves, because there isn't anything there to make out of yourself but a poor back grubbing slave for the likes of Jonah, for him to go to Whitleyville and brag about how he's going to have a good crop because you can make a good crop but you aren't smart enough to ever own anything of your own. Well, I'll tell you what I'm going to do. I'm going to get a job. I don't know what it's going to be, but as long as I can breath, I can earn a living and I will put something away and someday, I'm going to have something to call my own and it isn't going to be from the hands of Jonah!"

"We've got two girls coming on, to feed. They are already seeing things they want and asking for them, and I don't have the heart to just say they can't have them."

"Well, there's more to life than wanting things and when they get old enough, they are going to want things whether they see them or not. There is more hope for them here than there and I've said all I'm going to say and I've listened to all I'm going to listen to. I am not going anywhere, but to get me a job!"

I always knew Daddy intended to return to Tennessee. This job was only a temporary means to further his chance for a new kind of life there, but I knew that with a child's understanding. Temporary, for me, was a long time! Daddy had not saved money long enough to realize his land owning dream and now Mama seemed only to have shared the owning-something-of-her-own part of that dream.

Daddy was held in the firm grip of Tennessee land ownership. The touch and thought of rich, loamy soil brought a contemplative countenance to his face that was seen at no other time. Mama's thoughts of Tennessee soil brought a far different response: a vision of baking hot sun, sick fainting spells, hoeing dry furrows that stretched behind her and seemingly never-ending furrows laying ahead of her. She had no interest in farm work, other than interest in staying alive. Unknown to Daddy then, and only vaguely shaping itself in Mama's mind now, was an old but deep difference.

I knew this kind of talk did not bode well for me. I had been on uncertain ground since we left the hollow, trying to find a place to fit in. Now school had become that place and I ached at the thought of being taken from it! Being taken up with school thoughts, and not hearing Mama's and Daddy's daily talk, had spared me much misery; I wished I had never overheard the words that were just spoken! It mattered not whether I had heard them, the feelings were there.

In a few days, Daddy was called back to work but the silence between him and Mama was loud! I knew Mama would be looking for a job, although she never said a word about where or when she was going to look for it. She never became excited about something before it happened. Mama was that way. For her, there would be time to get excited when something did happen. She told me there might be a day, when I got home from school, that she would not be at home. She told me I was to stay in the apartment until Sister came home from her school and then the two of us were to continue sitting in the apartment until she got home. She didn't know I'd overheard the worrisome conversation between her and Daddy.

I could not know what kind of work Mama would find but if she found a factory job, I knew she would be just as at home making airplanes as she was sewing lace insertion for ribbons on one of my dresses. I felt there was nothing Mama couldn't do! She had done brave things in Tennessee and there too, she had told me to sit still and not move an inch until she got home. In Tennessee, a sow with a new litter of pigs rooted on the same path that Sister walked to school. Mama walked with her carrying a stick to protect them. Before leaving with Sister, Mama put two sweet potatoes in the fireplace ashes and told me to watch them and not move an inch until she got back; we would eat the sweet potatoes for our dinner. I was used to Mama telling me to sit still and wait until she came home. I sat unmoving, although now there were no roasting sweet potatoes nor a sow to keep me there. I would be in the same spot when Sister came home from school.

Sister and I talked while we waited: not about paper dolls or reading stories, but about Mama and Daddy, his job and the eminent possibility of leaving Detroit and returning to Tennessee. The impending uncertainty of the times and our family's circumstance weighed heavily upon us; we were vulnerable, innocent girls without power to effect anything. Our youth collided with world and family turmoil. A certain cruel wisdom pervaded our young minds and years. We saw and felt Mama's and Daddy's misunderstandings but could do nothing except talk to each other. The conflicts between Mama and Daddy, seemed to us, more than living here or there or even a job or the lack of a job. They felt much deeper. Even if the things we had heard and feared were resolved, it felt like there would still be disagreement between Mama and Daddy. Sister tried to help me with the hurtful underlying uncertainty that filled all the spaces inside me, by telling me not think about it. She said Mama's and Daddy's anger would go away, then everything would be as it was before I had heard their conversation. I wanted to believe her.

Mama found us where she had asked us to wait. While gone from the house, she had gotten a job at the Hudson Motor Factory. She would work during the day, sewing airplane seat covers. Since Daddy worked during the afternoons and evenings, there would be one and a half hours between the time Daddy would leave for work and the time she would return from work. During that one and a half hours, mine and Sister's directions were the same; stay in the apartment and go nowhere until Mama returned home. Sister was given the job of starting dinner and I was to help if needed. Mama would start work in two days.

CHAPTER EIGHT
The Piano Plan

I had played outside with my friends after school before Mama got a job, but after getting her job I had to wait inside the house until she came home. By the time Mama came home, my friends had gone inside. Mama told sister and me it was for our good that she was working, and we were helping her and Daddy get ahead by minding her. She told us how important it was that we study hard in school, learn everything they taught us, and most of all, make something out of ourselves! 'Making-something-out-of-ourselves' was a phrase Mama used over and over. I remembered her telling Daddy that there was nothing anybody could make out of themselves in Tennessee! I couldn't figure out exactly what she meant, but I was sure it had something to do with earning a living since she always spoke those words when she was talking about work and money.

While in the apartment waiting for Mama to come home, I began thinking about Gloria and how she practiced the piano from one to three hours a day. She never went outside to play right after school, for that was her practicing time. I began to think how much I wanted to play the piano too, the way Gloria played.

I had seen an upright piano in the front hall of my great aunt's house, but I had never heard anyone play it. I began to make a plan for getting that piano for my own but it was not easy to find a time to talk to Daddy about Gloria's piano playing and my possible piano ownership. My plan seemed small compared to the urgencies of others but I continued to wait and think. There had been a time for buying War Bonds in school. Mama and Daddy always liked the idea of saving money so they gave money to Sister and me to buy Government Savings Stamps. Each week we took the money, bought our savings stamps, and pasted them in our War Bond stamp book. When the books were filled, we visited the bank and were given a Certificate of Ownership for the bond. The bonds were in twenty-five dollar increments. I did not know about bond maturity, a ten year wait before our bonds would be worth twenty-five dollars! At the time we took them to the bank, we had only pasted eighteen dollars and seventy-five cents worth of savings stamps into the books! I had two books. In my mind, I had two twenty-five dollar War Bonds or fifty dollars!

I had been consumed with the piano idea as I had been with the beginning of school. I had been inattentive to the unfolding talk of the war's end. All the grown-up talk now was that the war was going to end very soon. I could feel their excitement and see it in their eyes. My aunts awaited my Marine Uncles' return, as did my aging grandparents. Many times I heard family members say my ailing grandmother would not live to see her two sons return from war. Their prediction proved right. My grandmother died on February 25, 1944 before my uncles were discharged on December 31, 1945. My uncles' courage in war had provided me with courage in my own small way. If they, I reasoned, could suffer things I'd heard Mama talk of, then surely I could bear up under the dentist's drill! At times, we heard they were hungry. This was particularly hard on Mama and Daddy for no matter how difficult the struggle to provide food had been, they had always managed that struggle, and the wartime factory job had quieted Daddy's immediate fears of being unable to earn a livelihood. However, it was difficult for me to reconcile the fact that our life had been made easier because of the war. It seemed too much of an unjust reality.

I was meeting the challenge of living in a new place, attending a new school, becoming accustomed to people with new ways and learning a new way of speaking. Prospects of the war's ending presented my most dreaded threat. I would most likely have to return to the very place that had been so difficult to leave. Talk of the war's ending abounded. People said it would end within weeks! Everybody was saying Germany was going to surrender. On May 7, 1945, Germany surrendered and signed the surrender terms. Our family, along with other renters in the boulevard house, was at the edge of Mrs. Rich's front porch to watch the VE Day, Victory in Europe, parade. We watched the grand parade move, at once slowly and then again fitfully, down East Grand Boulevard. It seemed the entire collection of paraders was being swept by a giant and invisible broom down the boulevard toward East Jefferson. Regiments of Scottish Bagpipe players, police platoons and National Guard troupes marched down the street. Many people shouted and waved American flags. Along its edges, the parade picked up jubilant participants, like blowing bits of waste paper gathered in by the giant broom. All the while, the plaintive drone of the bagpipes bound all other sounds together. The release of unexpressed fear and grief poured itself out in laughter, tears and animated body movements. Arms waved wildly as if to say, 'my voice is not enough,' I must speak with all of me and even then there will be much left unspoken. Happiness abounded, yet I felt great sadness. If the war was ending, Daddy would be going back to Tennessee and what would happen to me and my plan for piano lessons and to 'make-something-out-of-myself'? These mixed up feelings of three years colored my day and the days to come. I was a child of wartime and now of peacetime; for me, both realities were difficult.

It was at lunchtime, several days after the parade, when I got the chance to talk to Daddy about my plan to buy the piano. My lunch was waiting when I arrived home from Field school; Daddy had made it while making his own, which he packed into his black metal lunchbox. I ate while he sat with me. After eating, he would leave for his 'afternoon' shift job, and I would walk back to Field School. There was little time to tell Daddy about the piano I had seen in Aunt Daisy's front hall but I abruptly began. "I figure fifty dollars will be enough to buy the piano in Aunt Daisy's hall." He looked at me questioningly. "I want to take lessons and learn to play the way Gloria plays." He asked where I would get the fifty dollars I had mentioned. I told him about the two War Bonds I owned, also how hard it was just to sit and wait for Mama to come home. "If I had a piano I could practice like Gloria and I would have something to do while I waited for Mama." I added, "I think it will be a way for me to begin making-something-out-of-myself!" Daddy looked at me for a long time. He rested his elbows on the kitchen table and held his forehead with his fingers and wrapped his broad thumbs around his temple. After a long time of thinking, he said he would talk with my aunt about the piano.

All the urgency pushing inside me was poured out onto Daddy. Even though I had only asked for help in getting the piano, there was something deeper working its way out. The piano idea was fuller than I could tell Daddy. I wanted to learn to play the piano because there was a force building inside me that could not find release. I felt, by learning to play the piano, I could say things I could not say with words. I had diligently tried to master speaking words that told what I felt but I still could not speak all my feelings and knowings. I thought the music could say those things. Mama knew the feelings but she did not have the words for them either. We saw and felt a beauty and a sadness we had no words for. Beauty surrounded us in the hollow, but we never spoke of it, only saw and felt it. I wanted to tell about the things that Mama and I had not been able to speak. At the creek, we once watched black-green moss pulled by the water's force from soaked tree bark. The creek stretched the moss out and drew it down stream. The ruffled moss wavered in the water long enough for the sun to paint its edges with brightness. We didn't say a word but our eyes met with a knowing look of the unspeakable beauty of that moment. We both knew it had not gone unnoticed. I wanted to give that vision a voice.

Everybody in our family kept quiet about everything. Nothing was spoken, not even words about, what I felt, was the immediate return to Tennessee! I knew I was putting Daddy in a hard place, for the piano plan required money for lessons. Hadn't I heard him tell Mama he didn't have the heart to say no when we asked for things? I felt my urgency was greater than the urgency of his goal. If he got the piano for me, I felt sure these stirrings would be quieted. We continued with the arrangement of Mama working her shift and Daddy working his. Sister and I stayed close to each other after school and did what we had been told. School was the brightest part of my day but I worried that it and the new piano plan could disappear, the way Daddy had disappeared when he rode out of the hollow the day he left Tennessee for Detroit. I was accustomed to silence but I wanted a peaceful silence.

I remembered other quiet times overflowing with burdens. Our Tennessee church baptisms took place at the edge of the creek. I recalled the sound of crunching gravel as it moved under my feet and pushed against my ears when our small congregation walked nearer to the creek's edge for a closer view of the person being baptized. The preacher, carefully and slowly, lowered the person into the water until they were completely immersed. As he raised the person from the water, the congregation sang in hushed voices, "Are you weak and heavy-laden, cumbered with a load of care? Precious Savior, still our refuge take it to the Lord in prayer." The song's words echoed in my thoughts and prompted me to do as they had said.

CHAPTER NINE
Piano Lessons

Weeks passed and Daddy never mentioned the piano. He said he would talk to my aunt and I knew he would keep his promise. Although I had heard nothing, my thinking was filled with doubts—maybe she didn't want to sell it, maybe she would not accept the fifty dollars, maybe Mrs. Rich would not allow it in the apartment, even though she had invited me to sit at her long low piano whenever I silently looked at it. The light of my hopes grew dim, but it never went out. I could not understand how Mama could never became excited about something until it happened.

On a Saturday, when he was not working, Daddy told me some men would be coming in a few minutes with the piano. I would need to stay out of the way, he said, because it was very heavy and the back hall was narrow. It would be hard getting the piano into our apartment! It took four men to move the massive old upright piano through the narrow hall and into our small apartment. It was all I could do to keep myself out of the way of the moving men. The minute they got the piano through the back door and there was a space large enough for me to slip through, I went outside and quickly picked up the yellowed and chipped ivories that had fallen from the keys in the moving. I took them to the kitchen sink and began washing them. I rubbed and polished and rubbed some more, waiting for the men to leave so I could glue them back on the keys. Daddy and the four men walked to the outside where I heard the men say they didn't want to be around if we ever decided to move that piano again!

When Daddy returned to the room, he found me sitting at the piano gluing the ivory covers back on the keys. The uncertain feeling of not knowing if I would get the piano, was replaced with equally strong feelings of relief and gratitude. The piano was large and rendered even less space in the already crowded room, yet to me the room felt spacious and flooded with sunshine! While Daddy watched me glue the ivories back on the keys, he said he wanted to hear me play some hymns real soon.

Gloria had gotten permission for me to visit, observe her lesson and meet her teacher. I walked the distance from our apartment to the studio of Gloria's teacher, Mrs. Noack. Two wide, dark walnut double doors opened into the studio from the building's entrance hall. Only one door was used, leaving the other to form a deeply rich paneled inside wall. Two black grand pianos were positioned in the center of the room, in such a way that when sitting at them the pianists faced each other. Large framed posters of Toulouse-Lautrec's Moulin Rouge scenes hung on dark green painted walls; I would not know the name of the painter or the scenes until years later. Cabinets, storing new music, stood against one wall and a long low couch set against the other wall. Two softly lit lamps set on tables at each end of the couch. When sitting at the piano, one looked through floor to ceiling leaded glass French doors opening onto a concrete terrace with concrete balustrades forming a low wall around the terrace. Beyond the terrace, a grassy lawn sloped down and met East Jefferson Avenue with its passing automobiles. Only exhilarating silence in anticipation of the piano's sound was heard inside.

Mrs. Noack's teaching and playing moved beyond the walls of the studio and right into that newly awakened place in my being. I wanted to begin that day, that moment! I thought if only Mama could have been at the lesson, she too would have felt the way I did! How could it be that eyes and brains learn to read rows of notes forming the language of music, that fingers can be directed to depress keys releasing expressions of a soul's voice? Reading music was a great mystery to me but I was sure, with Mrs. Noack's help, I could solve that mystery.

My young and recently awakened yearnings were embodied in Mrs. Noack. She listened as I told her how much I wanted to learn to play the piano; she continued listening while I told her all the sounds and visions I had heard and seen and wanted to turn into music. She listened as if she had known me all my life and had heard my thoughts. She moved and spoke in a way that revealed, to me, deep convictions about music and grounded confidence in herself. The way she played the piano told me that playing was her other language. She asked which pieces I had liked in Gloria's lesson and if I had ever studied music. After my simple answers, it was agreed that I would talk with my parents and tell them the details: twelve dollars a month for a one hour lesson each week, payable at the end of each month, practice at least one hour each day and call back for a starting time if all was agreeable with Mama and Daddy.

Although I had not knowingly laid out a step-by-step plan, steps of a plan were unfolding. My plan had moved slowly but steadily. The seed of the idea had finally sprouted by having the old piano setting in our apartment and now Mrs. Noack had agreed to teach me. To tell Mama and Daddy about the lessons was the next step! After all, Daddy had said he wanted to hear me play hymns, and I had explained to him how much I wanted to take lessons! The twelve dollars a month loomed large but I would keep talking slowly and decidedly. This next step, the lessons, was the completion of the plan. It had to work.

Mama's and Daddy's dinner table talk had always been a barometer telling me how they were feeling toward each other and about certain other things. If things were going well, Daddy would often tell Mama she was 'right' about such and such a thing, meaning it had turned out the way she had said it would. I had silently wished that I too, someday, would say something that Daddy would say I was 'right' about. For me, he put an approval on what was said in a way others couldn't.

At the Sunday dinner table, I told them I had observed Gloria's lesson and met her teacher, Mrs Noack. After the first few words, a long stream of talk spilled out of me telling all that had gone on in my head and at Gloria's lesson. I even told Mama that if she had been there, I knew she too would have felt the way I did. I told them the price of the lessons and kept right on talking. I told them how the studio was so close I could walk by myself and—Daddy interrupted with, "I think you were 'right' about wanting that old piano. I believe you are going to do real well, and we can find the money somehow if you work real hard at learning to play. Maybe you too can help to pay for the lessons sometimes."

From the first time I saw the stacks of yellow music books on Gloria's piano, I had imagined possessing them. I was secretly disappointed when Mrs. Noack handed me my first book. It had a blue cover and was titled, *First Melody Lessons for Piano* by Mathilde Bilbro. I was soon to learn the color of the cover was the least thing I needed to be concerned about. *First Melody Lessons for the Piano* proved a challenge I had to reach for.

While I waited for my lessons to begin, and listened to the advanced student's lessons, I realized Mrs. Noack taught my beginning lesson as attentively and carefully as she taught the others. I was older than the other beginning students, but I kept my sight on what it would be like when I played the way the advanced students played. I held my music in my lap remembering the places that were difficult and the places I could play well. Anticipation before each lesson fed all my faculties with a ripe and tender readiness. As the lessons progressed, understanding between Mrs. Noack and me grew into a wholeness I had yearned for.

Within the first year, I was taught scales and exercises, given a new solo piece and a red exercise book, but the symbol I had waited for had not yet come. During a memorable lesson, when my time was almost finished, Mrs.

Noack walked to her music cabinet, took out a new book and returned to the piano where I was sitting. She placed the familiar yellow book on the piano. She said she thought I was ready for a new book. Pischna Technical Studies was my first *Schirmer's Library of Musical Classics* book! As time passed, the yellow cover became worn more from holding and looking at it than it did from practicing the exercises in it. It became a symbol of life's progression from idea to fruition. Within it's yellow covers were 'Sixty Progressive Exercises', but they represented another kind of progressive exercise only I could know!

I had thought of our family like Tennessee's Honeysuckle that grew so profusely and flourished along the road but I was still waiting for us to take root and flourish in Detroit. School provided a fullness I had never known but my new contentment was a tenuous thing. I constantly felt the shadow of Daddy's plan; we would return to Tennessee. It had been five years since we left the hollow and he had saved money, as he planned, but he had not planned for any changes in his family. Much of the five years in Detroit, I had longed for the hollow and all we left behind. Now, I found myself wanting this new life in Detroit and feeling threatened it would abruptly disappear. The urgency I had felt to stay in Detroit, until I could take care of myself, became so strong I prayed for the continuation of the war. I was that selfish!

Mama still had her job and spoke little about anything. She liked my interest in the piano yet her excitement I had hoped for was not there. I felt like learning music was a miracle, but Mama didn't act as if she felt it was. What I could not know then, was that piano playing was part of my plan to make something out of myself. It was not part of Mama's plan for herself. I didn't know if she had a plan, there was no way of telling. The knowing look of years ago, in our briefly fixed glances at the creek, was gone. Years later, I found a note, handwritten by Mama in the margin of her only school book, "...urged by a restless longing, she went her way sorrowing." In retrospect, I feel that quote characterized most of Mama's days in those years.

What I knew, but would not understand for decades to come, was that Mama had little to call her own. As a young girl, she was not allowed to go to school regularly. She was kept at home as the oldest child of eight to help my ailing grandmother with small brothers and sisters. If any time was left, she farmed like a hired hand. Mama's inclinations were toward thinking and learning. She was curious, bright and creative. A hilly Tennessee farm in the early years of the twentieth century was not a place for Mama's disposition. She had little chance to realize anything for herself and her yearnings. Daddy too, had little of his own in his young life but he did not behave as if he longed for something unspoken the way Mama did.

When Daddy spoke of having a place back home, one where he could have a fine garden and a fine house, Mama's reply was that he always wanted his head stuck in the dirt! They simply could not see and feel what the other saw and felt.

One of Mama's yearnings was reading. When she was a young girl and her family went to bed at the onset of dark, she stuffed quilts under the door of the room where she slept so the kerosine lamplight for her page would not betray her. The lamplight was discovered and both it and the book were taken from her; her duty was to sleep, to be rested for work in the fields the next morning. Even as an adult with her own young family, she found little time to read.

However, I could not understand Mama's feelings toward me. It felt like jealousy was keeping her from being happy for me. I was starting out in life and I did have more time and opportunity, however small, than Mama had. Her struggle to keep her factory job and her underlying reflections of her own life drained energy from her in a way that left little time to take joy in me and my quests. Mama had lived a long time with little hope, therefore the hope she saw in her factory job, with its small financial compensation, was something she wanted to keep. I entered adolescence with predictable convictions that my needs were more important than anybody else's and I had a powerful resolve to make my own way, so that in adulthood I could and would take care of myself. All these knowings shaped themselves into a silent and invisible wedge between Mama and me and between Daddy and Mama.

CHAPTER TEN
A Family Changed

When summer came, Daddy had made a vegetable garden on about ten square feet of ground in the backyard at the boulevard house. Spring simply could not come without Daddy putting out at least a few tomato seeds. Mrs Rich enjoyed seeing his neat rows of spaded earth and carefully spaced plants reaching for the sun. Each morning, before any sound of life came from the house, Daddy could be found on his knees, as if in prayer, pulling any weeds that were foolish enough to have sprouted in his garden. The feel of soil brought him, I think, the same satisfaction the piano brought me. The garden and soil were his other language.

Daddy had been willing to sacrifice living away from the place he loved, to make it possible to return to it in the way he wanted it to be. Five years of lifting heavy tires at the U.S. Rubber plant brought him money but not satisfaction, not the way the soil did. He felt he had earned the right to return to Tennessee. After all, wasn't that the reason he rode out of the hollow and left us all standing behind? In the progression of time, Sister and I were growing up and Mama's job had allowed her to discover life without farm work. Our hopes now no longer matched our hopes when we moved to Detroit. Mama and Daddy had not talked about their direction and I felt the pulling apart just like I had felt Daddy pulling the reins of the mule when I rode behind him.

Sister was almost eighteen years old and had fallen in love with a young man named Jack. I did not understand that kind of love, although I had seen a moving picture at the Whittier Theater on East Jefferson about what I thought was that kind of love. I had seen men and women's faces, on the large movie screen, kiss each other, and I saw Sister kiss Jack when I looked out the bathroom window on to our back porch. As I watched her, I felt she was grown up and was old enough to take care of herself, something I was not. Since she and I talked very little about things other than Mama's and Daddy's quarrels, I was surprised when she told me she was going to get married. She told me Mama was against it, but she was going to get married anyway. She was making decisions I could not make at thirteen. When I was younger, she read stories to me as many times as I had asked, she told me not to worry about Mama's and Daddy's disagreements, and stayed in the apartment with me while we waited for Mama. I didn't know where she would go once she was married, I only knew she would no longer be with me. Daddy had waited for the war to end and was going to return to Tennessee and Mama had told him she was not going to grub in the Tennessee dirt anymore. Where would Mama go? Where would I go? If I thought life was shaken like the numbers in the cakewalk drawing before we left the Wilmore Hollow, I was learning that life was still being shaken.

Mrs. Noack was my first thought when I needed someone to talk with. The lamps' soft light on either end of the couch in her studio made the rest of the darkened room seem warm and comforting. At the beginning of my lesson, after I told her I had not practiced the amount of time I should have, she asked if I could stay a while and talk after my lesson. She said she would have some time then. I was often convinced she knew my thoughts. I wanted more than anything to talk but right then! I had a way of spilling forth with talk if things got too filled up inside me. Mrs. Noack listened. She said we needed a plan to help me reach another challange, like *Mithalde Bilbro's First Melody Lessons*. She told me she could tell I would do very well with my music studies. She said she thought I could earn my living by doing something that required music. She said she thought I could teach, or teach something that required the knowledge of music. She told me we must start thinking along those lines and we would talk again, very soon, about how best to go about it. The warmth of her caring was reflected throughout the studio and in me.

When I began the seventh grade at Barbour Intermediate School, I knew nothing about the overall educational opportunities within the Detroit Public Schools. I had been content to go to school each day and as Mama said, "Do everything they tell you to do, learn everything there is there for you to learn and above all, make something out of yourself!" My sense of direction for the future had been the resources I found within my reach one day at a time. I hung on desperately to the vague notions I had concerning 'someday' but I did not know how to deliberately make those vague notions part of a plan.

During our next talk, Mrs. Noack told me she had been thinking about a special high school for me. She told me it was not a neighborhood high school where I could walk but rather, it was downtown, it was Cass Technical High School. She said there was a very fine music department there and I would get the best training to allow me to go to college. She smilingly said, I would learn skills to 'make-something-of-myself.' She said the school was not for everyone, but for those who wanted, very much, to get the best education. If I was to be accepted, I would need to prove I could do the work required. It would be hard work! She said my grades had to be kept at B+ or above and that a music applicant must have studied an instrument at least two or more years to qualify. The two years I had before entering high school in the tenth grade, according to Mrs Noack, would be very important. She then said, "I feel you can accomplish all these things but it will take work and time." I knew I could work hard, but time was the element in the plan that was not mine to control. I did not know if I had two days or two years in Detroit.

Had I known how to think about such things at thirteen, I would have been comforted by the idea that life can be seen as a kaleidoscope; the picture can be dramatically changed by the smallest turn of a single piece of colored glass. My idea of life was that of the farmer's: concerns of seasons, soil, weather and how they affect growing crops. Those concerns pervaded my farmer-father's being and that of mine in the way rains pervade the earth and water roots. My roots of thinking about life had been watered by anxiety, doubt and worry. I would now learn that life too can change by the smallest turn of an event.

Mrs. Noack knew about present time, and that it must be used fully if one is to have genuine concerns about future time. Her perspective of time was tempered by a life very different in kind than mine. Mrs. Noack's explanations of both present and future time-concerns were a revelation to me. Past time had been holding sway over me. The present was precisely where Mrs. Noack and I would began with our plan.

I was to make sure I enrolled in classes in intermediate school required for the classes I would need to take in high school. I was to enroll in the high-school classes required for the program I would follow in college. This was today's plan, and I was beginning the seventh grade! A taste of confidence had begun to grow within me at Field Elementary School; I felt it stir and awaken as I talked with Mrs. Noack and it kept me on the path she laid out for me.

During my appointment with the intermediate school counselor, who was to chart my classes each year, I told him precisely what Mrs. Noack and I had decided. I told him of my intention to attend Cass Technical High School. He noted those intentions in capital letters across the top of my folder and told me when the time came for me to talk to a representative from Cass Technical High school, he would be sure to call me to his office. All was settled at school, and I pretended the shadow of leaving Detroit did not exist. Of course pretending something did not exist did not mean it didn't, it was simply a means of putting my attention on something to hope for, so I would be able to live with the fear of the thing I dreaded—leaving Detroit.

CHAPTER ELEVEN
From Duplex to Flat

Daddy listened with interest, while his US Rubber Company friend told him about a flat, available for rent, on St. Clair Street. The flat was roomier than the boulevard apartment, he said, and the rent was comparable. The flat's German landlord, who lived upstairs, wanted a family who would care for the place as he had cared for it. He and his wife were aging and wanted someone to keep the lawn and small backyard garden in the manner they had kept it. They wanted someone who would take care of minor repairs and generally look after the place as if it was their own. This opportunity appealed to Daddy, especially the garden part. His friend had told the owner that he knew just the family he was looking for.

I never knew when the threads of understanding, acceptance and circumstance wove their logic into the fabric of Daddy's thinking and labeled that logic 'willing sacrifice' rather than 'defeat'. I know it had been a trying and troubling time for him. When the opportunity to rent the St. Clair flat presented itself, he must have been ready to say yes because he had already agonized over the realization that his dream of returning to Tennessee, must be changed. He would move to the flat but it would not be his last move in Detroit. He was now fashioning his dream on Detroit home ownership but that would take time. He had heard my plea and certainly knew Mama's feelings. He also knew that Sister would be married in a few months and would be making her own decisions. Daddy rode from the hollow for the good of his family, now he would stay in Detroit for the good of his family. I had seen my family's struggle in Detroit through my own eyes but I was beginning to learn that I had not been alone with my struggle. In their own way, Mama's and Daddy's struggle had been as desperate as mine.

Piano lessons and school were providing a rootedness I was hoping for in Detroit. However, my new contentment had been a layer of being that I alone knew, for I felt it had not been acknowledged by my family. I had constantly felt the shadow of Daddy's plan to return to Tennessee. It had been five years since we left the hollow and he had saved the money he planned. He constantly pondered his reasons for sacrificing the land he loved for his factory job. I had thought I would be living with uncertainty for an uncertain amount of time but this new move to the St. Clair flat would prove me wrong.

During our move from 177 East Grand Boulevard to the flat at 2564 St. Clair, the man whom I had observed in the upstairs hall, carrying an arm full of books, came to our apartment to tell us good-bye and wish us well. He carried a small black book which he put in my hand and said he hoped someday I would read it. As I held the thin book, I realized my top stair perch had not hidden me as carefully as I had thought. It would be sixty-three years before I read the small black book, Sherwood Anderson's *Poor White*. Thinking back, I was humbled to think the man, who had given me the book, had seen my family as the struggling Americans who peopled Sherwood Anderson's story. The encroaching industrial world was testing the resolve of thousands of families, not only ours. I think he had thought of us as we were in our Tennessee world without ever having been there. Mrs Rich also came to the apartment carrying two gifts, a framed photograph of her bull dog, with his father, along with a silver plated fruit stand. They were touching gifts from caring people who had lived in near proximity for the past five years. I was glad to know the extent of their care for us.

For many years after our move, the house at 177 East Grand Boulevard remained home to families whose names I no longer know. As time passed and circumstances changed, many returned to Tennessee where their tightly held dream, of land and home ownership, was realized. Others, like Daddy, made the agonizing decision to remain in Detroit and make a commitment to life in the North, for the sake of their families.

Sometime in the 1970s, 177 East Grand Boulevard, witness to decades of war time struggles, crumbled under the hands of a wrecking crew. With the house's falling, its purpose seemed to have been achieved. The post war years did not hold the need for its shelter as did the war years. In the future, its hardwood beams will still be identifiable by tree name but not place, the glass shards from its windows and cupboard doors will remain shards for centuries but the place of their standing will be unclear, its plaster dissolved with the elements into the earth and with that final dissolution, the house's exit was complete. For me, it is the site of lasting significance. The place, although fraught with much uncertainty, was a place of growing, a place where dreams were dreamed and the life sustaining qualities of discovering, imagining, observing and learning were realized.

CHAPTER TWELVE
A New House and a New Sense of Self

When I walked through the new flat's front door at 2564 St. Clair, I sensed a feeling of being equal to my friends. Now we could enter my house, as well as their's, through a front door. The painted gray back door entry at the boulevard house had colored my thirteen year old sense of worth, painted it grey and left me sensitive to not having an entrance like my friends. In time, I learned the shifting and altering feelings within me were called 'growing up' but then, I watched life's inchoate panorama with wide-open eyes, feeling every subtle change demanded my response. I would come to know, as I grew older, that life's sorrow, loss, and fear are responses to life's events and they can be painted with a brush dipped in pigments deep within myself. To mix those pigments thoughtfully and thoroughly would be one of life's most exacting tasks.

I was excited to have a bedroom to call my own. Mama and Daddy would occupy the bedroom off the kitchen, and sandwiched between it and the front bedroom, that was Sister's and her husband Jack's, was the small room I would call mine. The single bedroom window was about three feet from the flat next door and very little light entered it. Because of that closeness, we would later learn that our landlady, living in the upper flat and her upper flat next door neighbor, often exchanged pies and other baked goods, set on a broom and passed through their kitchen windows.

With Daddy's help, I set about making my room my own. He covered a wood frame with dark green plastic material and made a special headboard for my bed. We moved the small dresser, that had been stored at my Aunt's in Tennessee since the move from the hollow, into my room. I set up a desk area on a card table where I neatly stacked books, especially the giftbook from the man upstairs at the boulevard house, and writing materials. With paint and my imagination for window curtains, the small room became, for me, a magazine picture. I immediately felt at home in the flat.

We rarely heard sounds from Mr. and Mrs. Krause upstairs. He and Daddy got on in a happy, congenial way, both being fastidious in their work habits and taking delight in gardens. Mama too was happy in her new surroundings and through talk of cooking and household chores, made friends with Mrs. Krause. Mama had an outside clothes line again and hung the clothes in the sun. It seemed like a big, happy family with the quiet couple upstairs and our family downstairs. Each day was marked by a settled rhythm. Sister and her husband had jobs and went off to work. Mama would keep her factory job only a few more weeks before she would be laid off; the Hudson Motor Company would no longer make airplane seat covers. She would stay home during the day doing the daily housework she knew so well. I looked forward to coming home from school where I found her, listening to the radio, while ironing or cooking dinner. Daddy went to work and I went to school, he taking two buses to the US Rubber Co. and I taking two buses to Barbour Intermediate School. The lonely days of waiting for Mama to come home and the turbulence of the Boulevard years seemed far away, or, was I growing far away from them?

Barbour Intermediate School proved to be a fertile place for my growing desire to learn and my imagination. Whatever idea I had at school, a need for that idea seemed to surface. Latin class was an expanding experience. Learning to translate Latin words into English became as exciting as learning to read music. The new awareness of a Latin root in an English word became an exciting discovery and often caused me to smile. Of course agricola, meaning farmer, would be the root word of agriculture. Latin class also seemed an unlikely place for my creativity, but I was mistaken. I was assigned a large, glass doored hall case where I displayed dolls from many nations, dressed in their native clothing, against a backdrop map of their countries and languages. The project involved doing all the things I loved most: access to unlimited art supplies, free reign to plan and carry out the project in the manner I chose and encouragement all the way. Fabric scraps to sew the doll's costumes, came from Mama's scrap supply. I found pictures and read stories about the countries and people I showed in my display and delighted in seeing pictures of other country's hills, trees, and rivers. A colored picture of the Appian Way, on the frontispiece in my Latin textbook, brought a feeling of familiarity, for I felt a closeness to those tall Cedars and that narrow road. My world became larger and my delight in it greater, especially when my learning connected visually to the place of my beginning.

My most satisfying class at Barbour was the music class. With the great number of students at school, two music teachers taught classes three days a week. One teacher taught basic music and singing while the other taught chorus, formed singing groups and planned concerts. The thrust of our year's learning was directed toward a performance at the school's Spring Festival. We sang in the three part harmony our young voices could accommodate and I was always excited about practicing on the stage of the school's large auditorium. The plain wood stage would be transformed when Spring Festival time came for we would have made small pink crepe paper blossoms by the thousands, twisting them on real life tree branches set on the stage as backdrop for our performance. It was the work and genius of inspired teachers to assign seventh and eighth grade boys the task of twisting pink crepe paper into apple blossoms, but the busywork worked! After our performance, chills of delight filled me as loud applause filled the auditorium.

The months leading up to ninth grade graduation were months of thinking about how the three years at Barbour Intermediate had been the first phase of the three phase plan of my long and important journey to 'make something out of my self.' The next three years, at Cass Technical High School, seemed formidable but the echo of Mrs. Noack's voice, "I'm sure you can accomplish all these things," was the encouragement that sustained me. During the past three years at Barbour, I was part of a singing group called the double quartet, four boys and four girls. We faithfully practiced our harmonizing parts for we had been asked to sing at our graduation. We chose the song, "You'll Never Walk Alone" from the 1945 Rodger's and Hammerstein musical, *Carousel*. The words were familiar to me, not from knowing the music or having heard them sung but from the past years of tightly holding to hope, having dreams tossed and blown and being afraid of the unknown. Singing the song confirmed my new found confidence in myself and the overwhelming confidence I had grown to know at school. The lyrics felt like they had been written for me. I sang the song with the belief that I would 'never walk alone'.

Now that we seemed settled in Detroit, Daddy's summer vacation time from factory work was spent 'down home.' In the years before 1949, the four of us would ride to Tennessee with someone Daddy knew who was driving to the same area our family lived. It was a long and tiresome drive. Roads were poor and directions always unclear. The only air came through opened windows constantly blowing hot, dry air on our faces. We often stayed overnight in a 'Tourist Home,' a private house where a room or two was rented to travelers if the driver became too tired or directions too unclear after dark. After an encumbered two days, we arrived at our aunt's and uncle's house to a warm and loving welcome. In 1949, Daddy was able to buy a new Plymouth car.

A joyous time began on our arrival in Tennessee. Word spread quickly when we would be coming 'home.' It was a time when Daddy sat and visited with his aging parents. We visited relatives and friends who remained in the

South and we visited the cemetery where the graves of family and friends were marked with new and ancient headstones. As I stood quietly on the grass covered ground, gathered with my parents and others around a family grave, I was filled with deep respect for the closeness and love in our large and long lived family. Those who had died seemed never to be forgotten. We visited their graves just as faithfully as we visited those still living. Even in our talks at twilight, many tales and references were made to members of our family in times long past. Large family gatherings convened around tables ladened with abundant, perfectly cooked, Southern Country food. Every dish of food on the table had been grown in the gardens and fields of my grandparent's farm. Chickens, from their pen, would have been dressed that morning for the evening meal. In the hot and humid summer evenings, after the large meal was eaten, my aproned aunts and grandmother sat around the vacated table, with tired, sweating faces cradled in their palms supported by elbows resting on the table. Their day's hard work of preparing dinner for as many as sixteen or more adults and many children, caught up with them and they sat for a lengthy time talking softly yet glowing because their family members were now 'home.'

Cousins ran around the house playing hide-and-seek or catching fireflies and putting them in canning jars, others swung on the porch swing pretending to travel to distant places in fast automobiles. In the twilight, our uncles and grandfather sat on slat chairs on the front porch or on chairs leaned back against an ancient Oak tree in the yard. They talked of crops, weather, new or old animals, often politics and especially the Secretary of Agriculture. The heavy heat of summer pressed down on everyone, slowing our speech and thoughts but the thoughts that were never slowed were those of Daddy. He always wrested with the ever present question, 'how is it, I can bring myself to leave all this I hold so dear?'

Many of those summers, I was allowed to stay on with my Dudney grandparents in Free State until September when school began in Detroit. Those days were filled with fleeting, joyous farm chores: sewing broomstick skirts from flour sacks saved for me by my grandmother, helping her iron, sweeping the inside of the house and front porch, running errands to the cellar or the smokehouse, and picking green beans and tomatoes. They were chores without heavy responsibility, but with the joy of pleasing my grandmother. We often sat around the kitchen table stringing green beans or shelling peas. I slept in what Grandmother called the lower room. It was a special guest room, special in that most of the extravagant gifts, satin comforters and fancy pillows from her children living in the North, were put on the bed in that room. My grandmother never woke me when the farm day's work began at

4:00 or 4:30 but I was awakened, in my lower room bed, slightly before dawn by the soft clucking and scratching sounds the roaster made outside the window. In perfect timing with the rising sun, the roaster's full blown crowing began. I ate my breakfast at the kitchen table while Grandmother washed the breakfast dishes from Granddaddy's breakfast and any other farming friend or family member who might have stopped for a hot biscuit with a spoonful of molasses. The minute the dishwater was thrown outside for chickens to drink, my grandmother began her daily dinner preparations. In late afternoon, she changed her work apron for a clean one and headed to the porch swing, where she and I would rest.

I often walked the rolling, graveled, Free State Road both in morning and moonlight with my distant cousin Patty Fuqua; our talks centered on my life in Detroit and her's in Tennessee and without our awareness of it, those sultry summers cemented a lifelong friendship. After those languid months, my return to Detroit required a poignant and abrupt readjustment. The pace of Detroit and school life quickly blurred that other 'home' feel of life in Tennessee.

Arriving home in September, to the St Clair flat, I learned that Mama and Daddy had bought a new house at 1605 Lappin! I knew they had been thinking about a new house after we had lived in the flat for a short while but I had not expected another move to come so quickly! I guessed the decision had been made while I was spending the summer in Tennessee. When the last bit of construction was completed on the new house, we would move in. Daddy's change of heart and direction of many months ago, made it possible for me to continue holding to my hoped-for plan; it appeared my plan was clearing yet another hurdle. Wanting to inspect the house and show it to me, Daddy drove Mama and me there on a day right after he arrived home from work. While Mama and Daddy showed me through the rooms and talked of their plans, a look of togetherness shown on their faces, a look I had not seen in many years. For me to embrace certainty, and expect that some years might stretch before me without foreboding circumstances, would be a new way of experiencing life. With the new house and our move into it on the horizon, I now felt certain I would be able to attend the three years at Cass Tecnical High School.

PART TWO

Detroit, Michigan Teenage Years
1949-1952

CHAPTER ONE
Arriving at Cass Technical High School

I was required to ride two buses and one streetcar for each one-way trip, a total round trip each day of two hours and twenty minutes to arrive at Cass Technical High school. The unreliability of public transportation schedules and my desire to be punctual, raised that total travel time each day to three hours to arrive on time; another seven hours were spent attending classes, practicing our instruments and attending rehearsals. Cass Tech, as it would be called now that I was a student, lay a little west of downtown Detroit and the public transportation I rode traveled into areas I had never seen. In the waiting time before transferring to the Second Avenue bus, I had a clear view of Woodward Avenue, Detroit's main downtown artery and address to many world class stores and businesses. Numerous streets ran east and west off Woodward and were address to hundreds more lesser known but equally intriguing shops and Fine Arts studios. By the time I arrived at school, my mind was filled to overflowing with sights and sounds of a large downtown city that, in the next three years, I would explore and embrace as my own.

I no longer remember if I attended an orientation program at the school before beginning classes but my clear recollection, of that first day, is standing in front of the building on Second Avenue, looking straight up to the top of its soaring seven floors, each floor a visible part of the dramatic Art Deco designed building. After entering, my attention was immediately drawn to exceptionally large framed graduation photographs, hanging in stately arrangements on high walls, of each graduating class since 1917. Hundreds of eager young faces showed visible convictions that their lives had been immeasurably enriched by the fact they had graduated from this unique school. To reign in my lofty thoughts, I devised a tally of dates; I calculated that in 1934, the year I was born, Cass Technical High School was seventeen years old. In 1949, the year I was entering, I was a little shy of two years less than seventeen years old. From the time its doors were opened in 1917 until 1949, it had stood through two World Wars fought on foreign land and a Great Depression gripping this land. I felt confident its students were lovers of liberty and I knew them to be students of freedom, with high aspirations for their's and their country's future.They had thoughtfully passed through these halls and faced their plans for the future, now it was my time to pass through the same halls and discover for myself what the passing would mean for my future. As was my habit, I suspect I was mentally piecing together a picture puzzle, attempting to find where my piece fit. After deducing as much meaning as I could from the physical aspects of the building, I gradually found my way to the sixth floor where the venerable music classes were held.

Instruction in the music department included the subjects of Harmony, Music Theory, Wind instruments, String instruments, Ensemble playing (orchestra, concert band, marching band and harp ensemble) and Choral music (choirs and small group singing). Since there was not a specific program for piano majors, we were required to become harp majors. I'm unclear how that thinking evolved but I was thrilled at the prospect of learning a new instrument, especially one so historically enduring and beautiful. I had heard stories about the harp in the Bible but the only time I had seen a harp was during a Field Elementary School field trip, of many years ago, to attend a Detroit Symphony Orchestra concert.

In my first harp class I was introduced to an aging and ill harp instructor named Miss Loretta Kink, who would retire a few weeks into the semester and be replaced by Miss Velma Froude; she remained my teacher for the next three years. Five Lyon and Healy pedal harps stood in the harp room. Other than the harps, the room was sparsely furnished except for a few chairs and music stands. Tall windows looked out the sixth floor harp room on an inner square space formed by the shape of the building.

First Harp lesson! "Sit, with feet flat on the floor and knees slightly apart, place the finger tips of each hand on the narrow piece of wood at the edge of the sounding board and slowly bring it back to rest on your right shoulder, not completely though for your knees should be helping you balance the eighty pound instrument." These instructions were given by Miss. Froude who proved to be an exacting and demanding teacher.She was opposite in every way to my beloved piano teacher. "Practice each of these movements until they seem natural and you have control of the instrument!" I was given a practice time of one hour daily at the harp. The practice times were to be faithfully kept, without change, so others could expect to have their scheduled time.

Second lesson. The music put in front of me was not unfamiliar; what was unfamiliar was the unusual markings with lines and numbers underneath each staff. I was to learn that every change in tone on each string of the pedal harp, had to be made by changing the position of one or more of seven pedals at the base of the harp; there were three notched positions for each pedal, each notch designated one of three tone changes: natural, flat and sharp. The numbers 1 through 4 gave instructions for the placement of fingers on the string, thumb and first three fingers only. The fifth finger was never used except for certain types of octave placement. The lesson continued at a very brisk pace with simple, though not yet to me, pedal changes. These lessons would continue for the duration of the semester. There would be one, one hour lesson each week, as well as the one hour daily practice time. I was told I would develop blisters on my playing fingers but that was to be expected and that would be a good thing for the blisters would become callouses making my fingers ready to 'play'! The pain between the blister and the callous stage was not addressed. The austerity of feeling in this introduction to the harp was overshadowed by my clouded romantic images of the instrument. I soon discerned the difference between my inflated perceptions and reality.

I was, however, beginning to see the complete seriousness and no-nonsense attitude toward undertaking a music education at Cass Tech. Not that I would have wanted it to be any less demanding but I did discover that not all instructors presented themselves or their teachings in the manner of Velma Froude.

CHAPTER TWO
Beginning Classes

As each class unfolded, music at Cass Tech proved mentally and physically (more about physically later) demanding. Music students were required to take a survey class in each type of instrument: string, wind and percussion. The survey classes were one semester each. The instructor's subjective assessment of the student's strengths or aptitudes, determined the particular instrument assigned. In the winnowing process, I was assigned cello for string, bassoon for wind, albeit was a reed wind instrument, and triangle and glockenspiel for percussion All instruments in the music department were stored in the instrument room under the watchful eye of Rodney Blood. Mr. Blood was a perfect choice for his job. Not only was he scrupulously attentive to the condition of each instrument but he repaired any needs the instruments presented. The room, a vault like place with steel storage shelves and racks, housed the instruments we checked out, as in library books, for our classes. The cello was certainly not as large as the stringed bass, but for me it was a heavy instrument to lift over the counter of Mr. Blood's instrument room. After checking out our instrument, we carried it on the crowded elevator from the sixth floor instrument room down to the main floor auditorium or a practice room anywhere it could be found on the sixth floor. The physically demanding part was taking the bassoon, in its cumbersome case, home to practice and back to school the next day on six different buses. It was heavy, expensive when reeds split and difficult in crowded buses. Harp was the instrument I was to become proficient on but they remained in the harp room.

After the specifics of the music classes were settled, I began to adjust to the reality of work in the academic classes: Latin, a continuation of Barbour Intermediate School Latin, English Literature, Geometry, History and Public Speaking. These were the classes for the first year. My time was filled with more studies and practicing plus traveling time than I could have ever anticipated, yet there was still time to enjoy many friends, for they too were as busy as I. Mary Beyers, whom I have remained close to for the past sixty years, was a close friend at intermediate school as well as Cass Tech and has remained so through all life's changes. At times, we were found practicing until 10:30 at night in the empty Cass Tech seven floor building and we would return the next morning for a similar time schedule to be repeated. All of this took place in the 50's when Detroit streets and public transportation travel after dark, was safe for a teenage girl.

Soon after the harp 'felt natural' and I was 'in control of the instrument.' I was put in the Harp and Vocal group and Harp Ensemble. The Harp and Vocal group was a group of about twenty-six female voices accompanied by three to five harps. Most of the time, Velma Froude was one of the accompanist as well as the music director. The Harp Ensemble consisted of five harpists who played musical arrangements ranging from classical to contemporary Broadway show music and sometimes religious music. Most of the music we played had been arranged for harp by Velma Froude. That music also became the music for our weekly harp lesson.

The new teachers and students, of untold personal and musical backgrounds, not to speak of their eye-opening exhibits of talent when performing, combined with venues great in diversity, going far beyond the walls of Cass Tech, stilled me in their uniqueness and intensity. In the heat of these new and telling experiences, I began to take inventory of my musical talents. I was still too young and too inexperienced to have full realization of what I was up against but I did begin to have new considerations for what my piano teacher had told me three years earlier; 'I'm sure you can make your living with music or a related field that involves music.' I began to consider, and would intensify that consideration of, the 'related field' part of her statement, although it was in retrospect, totally subconscious.

CHAPTER THREE
New Insights

During those times of introspect, I discovered a considerable talent that lay in an area other than music. I was asked to speak on many occasions: to introduce speakers, to speak on the radio station WDTR, Detroit's Public School radio station and to have speaking parts in radio plays. A serendipitous experience revealed itself when I was asked to have a reading part, on radio, in the play, *The Hundred Dresses*. That story had been the story I loved most in elementary school and the one I ask to hear many times over. I was asked to be president of the Harp and Vocal group and the Harp Club. That responsibility required frequent speaking opportunities. I still have in my letters, copies of very kind words from Cass Tech's Principle, Mr. William Stirton. My public speaking class was a new found interest and I relished in the new arena. There were many interdepartmental luncheons and award ceremonies. I was at a podium weekly in those days and was very pleased to be there. In later years I became amused at the speaking phase of my high school days and felt I must have been the only one my age to have had so many hours of speaking practice, albeit with paper dolls, and intense observation of other's speech. Although I would for many years, have difficulty with the spoken vowels of the northern tongue, saying pin for pen and pen for pin, I consciously spoke the unvoiced sounds in the learned way and my ear for speech continued to pay off.

To say the number of concerts held each year in the Cass Tech Music Department was ambitious, would be an understatement. Each division of the department held either a separate concert altogether or they combined with another division for a joint concert. There was Concert Band, Orchestra, Harp and Vocal, Choir and at times Marching Band concerts, not to speak of the numerous individual recitals and guest performances. Often the guest performer was a Cass Tech graduate who had gone on to greater levels of achievement but many times there were concerts of nationally renowned musicians. One particular occasion for the harp students, was the Detroit arrival of Carlos Salzedo. His harp recordings and performances were storming the music world because of previously unheard of special effects which he had perfected. He wove paper strips in the harp strings at the sounding board level, giving a crackled and non-resonate sound to particular sections of his own compositions. He thumped on the sounding board with knuckles and finger tips and used glissandos at a dizzying speed and repetition. He used his finger nails for another particular sound. He played a Lyon and Healy harp and because of his legendary effect on the harp world, the Lyon and Healy Company designed, in 1928, a special harp and named it the Salzedo Concert Grand. And grand it was with its red and silver stripes on Sitka Spruce. It was in the 1920's Art Deco style! I wondered when thinking back to that time if Mr. Salzedo had been made aware of the beautiful Art Deco design of the Cass Tech building. He was Philadelphia's Curtis Institute of Music's harpist in residence. More than fifty years later, I was thrilled to see his Salzedo Harp standing in a practice room with his name on the door at the Curtis Institute of Music. In his 1951 visit to Detroit, he shocked us with his short stature yet gargantuan personality. He was the Cass Tech harp department's 'close your dropped jaw' guest for three days. It happened that Velma Froude was a student of his in the summer sessions at the Curtis Institute and therefore had some inside influence for his guest appearances.

There were numerous school and social affairs concurrent with the ever growing number of concerts. For teen age girls, there was always the question, 'what will I wear?' From the time I had longed for the bolt of red Dotted Swiss at Ben Baugh's store in Gainesboro, Tennessee, I had loved the idea of sewing. Around the age of twelve, I began to sew for myself; I sewed simple broomstick skirts from flour sacks at first, then more complicated patterns. My 'what will I wear?'question was simultaneously replaced by, 'what will I sew?' I still marvel at the amount of activities I could pack into twenty-four hours. I was often found at the sewing machine at two o'clock in the morning and still sewing the last snap on a garment minutes before I left the house for an event. My mind was so taken with all life offered I slept little, except on the hour plus bus rides to and from school.

We were required to wear formal gowns at all Harp and Vocal concerts. I will comment here about the diversity of venue I spoke of earlier. Our many concerts were held in Detroit hotel ballrooms, civic auditoriums and any other venue where the sponsoring group wanted to showcase Cass Tech's musical talent. Many concerts were in combination with other school groups both local and state. Frequent concerts were by invitation from the

University of Michigan and Michigan State University, however, in those years, it was Michigan State College.

Sewing gowns for the many performances was yet another creative outlet. I simply could not sit still at that age. Life was far too exciting to let a minute of inactivity hinder progress toward some new goal. I mentioned earlier that I would embrace Detroit's downtown for my own and embrace it I did! My direct trip home from school was frequently interrupted to wander in the seemingly endless aisles of downtown Detroit's J.L. Hudson Co.'s fabric department. However as stellar as Hudson's was, I fell in love with Midwest Woolens, located on Broadway off Woodward. The fabric there was displayed by color, every range possible, plus hundreds of bolts turned on end in the center isles. It was a wonderland of fabric! The 'woolen' part of the store's name was a misnomer for there was every type of fiber one could think of, not only wool.

I had created costumes and clothing in my mind, for what seemed like my entire life. The first made garments, leaves joined by thorns, felt a long journey backward now that I was standing in a place where my mental creations could become realized! If I saved every penny from my part-time jobs, I could afford the fabric, for it was wholesale priced. I toted home bags filled with yards of netting, taffeta, cotton and velvet, spread them on the floor before me and delighted in my selections. I turned any vision or sight into a design idea: a passing blur of light suggested color combinations, a particular line, broken or straight lent itself to a garment shape. When the gown I had sewn was finished and I carried it to school for an afternoon performance, I knew there would be no other gown like mine! I've wondered, in my adult years, why that was so important to me, when I wanted to be like my friends in almost all other ways. In the 50's, dancing was a favorite social activity and there were numerous opportunities to dance to music performed by Cass Tech musicians, where I proudly danced in my personally sewn creations.

CHAPTER FOUR
Confusion to Clarity

On a particular evening, Cass Tech's auditorium house lights were out. The only light puncturing the deep dark space was the eery presence of the red Exit signs. They gave a patchwork look to the darkness. The stage lights, however, cast bright light on the five harps, four other students, Velma Froude and me. It was 10:30 in the evening on a week night; the Harp Ensemble had been practicing since about 6:30 p.m. New blisters had formed around the edges of the callouses on my fingers, making them very painful. Five of us were playing but there had been continued mistakes in our playing. It may have been a different player making a different mistake each time we played the piece but Miss Froude said we must all play the piece perfectly and in unison. If we did not, we would stay there until we did! My fingers hurt, I was tired and thinking that it would be midnight by the time I rode two buses and a streetcar home. I could no longer think of the music, only of going home. Uncharacteristic of me but strongly heard in my head, was at first a subtle but gradually louder voice clearly saying, 'I don't want to be here; I don't want to work this hard and in this way for this woman. This practice is not about my progress in playing the harp, it is about Velma Froude's ego. I don't care what the consequences of my leaving will be. I am going to get up, leave this stage, this harp, this teacher and go home. As I left the stage, Miss Froude called after me, "If you leave this practice, you will not play in tomorrow's concert and you will no longer play in the Harp Ensemble. You will be finished with the harp."

On the final leg of the trip home, I was still hearing Velma Froude's voice. "You will be finished with the harp." It had been two years since I had first seen the five harps standing in the harp room. I had been moved by their beauty and I had been willing to sacrifice time and great effort to learn to play the instrument. I had been a faithful and competent student and was grateful for the opportunity. This seemed a thankless and reckless way to end such a commitment. I was too tired to consider it further. I got off the bus and went home to bed.

In the clarity of the next new day, I thought again how nurturing Mrs. Noack had been in the early days of my music education at the piano and how unlike the harp lessons had been compared to those piano lessons. I also knew there had been something missing in the harp lessons that had been very present in the piano lessons. The piano lessons had been about me and my efforts. There was nothing about Mrs Noack in the lesson, except of course her masterful teaching. I also knew the missing element in the harp lessons. It was the absence of me and the great presence of Velma Froude. It was she who dominated the harp lessons and the harp performances. We, the students, were secondary. I began to think about the teaching process itself, the unmistakable value of a caring relationship between the teacher and student contrasted with the destructive disregard and unproductive power of an uncaring teacher toward a student. I was not remorseful about my decision of the night before, on the contrary, I was energized and pleased that such understanding and fortitude had surfaced. That evening's events and consequent decision was a turning point on my way to 'making-something-out-of-myself.'

For the past four years I had been following a path of music instruction and music performance, a path laid out for me by Mrs.Noack. It was a necessary plan, without it I would not be in the position to make other decisions now. I had been confident that the plan laid out for me would be the way to independence. By acquiring musical skills, I would at some point, be able to support myself. I had followed the directions faithfully, yet now there was a new clarity. After the incident with Miss Froude, at the late night rehearsal, I began thinking about the factors that had led me to this point. Music had been the conveyance to get me where I wanted to be and I had mistaken it to be the stopping point. Now I was beginning to understand that it was just that, a conveyance, not the ultimate goal. I had known for sometime that, as a performer, I was not on level ground to compete musically with the Cass Tech Music Department's talented students. Most of them had studied far longer than I and they had been greatly supported in their endeavors by their families. They had not struggled, I was quite sure, with the same circumstances I had struggled. I was maturing and gathering ideas from many people, far different from me, and all that knowledge was shaping itself into a force I was obliged to consider. I was beginning to understand that I could make decisions based on what I felt and discovered about myself. It would now be up to me to define the choice that would get me where I could support myself. I had stretched myself to test my abilities but I was also accepting my limitations. I was ready to make the necessary decisions.

I had a final year of high school to complete and within that year I would come to know the direction I was seeking. I thought carefully about the different teaching methods of the many teachers I had known. The idea of teaching held a strong sway over me. I had been able to discern good and ineffective teaching. I began to wonder whether I might become a teacher. I felt sure my convictions would equip me to be a helpful, caring and productive teacher. My speaking experiences had been helpful in many ways and I felt able to articulate ideas with confidence. I also felt teaching to be a highly regarded profession. I had heard of kindergarten teaching and I was curious to know more about it. I learned from Mrs. Noack that music was important, even required, for a kindergarten teacher at that time. There was great emphases, in those days, on the importance of the arts in teaching kindergarten aged children. At the time, a kindergarten teacher was required to play the piano, include drama and dance in her teaching and be able to discover and read fine children's literature to her students. She also needed to love art and be able to present art projects that were non competitive, ones that were designed with emphases on the process of creativity rather than the production of an object. The purpose was to foster individuality. Teaching kindergarten was to promote exploration and spur discovery and wonder in nature and in people. All of these aspects appealed to me because they reflected the way I had learned as a child and were the processes I had taken great delight in.

I began to think of all the learning I had experienced and realized that learning came about because of inspiring and inspired teachers with interest in an eager student. I had again developed a new goal without setting out to develop one. I had one more year to test my thinking. I did so in every situation I met. I began to understand that great teaching and learning was not confined to a class room. It was a state of being. Memory fed examples of this discovery. At Field Elementary, there were private explanations for long division in a caring and encouraging way, I had received motivating hand written thank-you notes from Mr. Stirton, Cass Tech's principal and been part of talks with our intuitive band instructor, Harry Begian. Those talks prompted personal discoveries that were not confined to band practice or instrument instruction. Mrs. Noack remained the supreme example of a nurturing teacher. My new understanding was that learning and teaching are inextricable. My previous understanding of my goal had changed direction. The compass of that understanding was no longer unsteady but pointed straight ahead; it made perfect sense. I would follow this dream of teaching and work until the dream turned to reality or I would find a better dream to replace it.

It had been a long journey from the Wilmore Hollow to the halls of Cass Technical High School, both in distance and time. Another long journey lay ahead—to attend and graduate from Wayne University's College of Education. I held the belief that if I saw the simple yet revealing truths in the world around me and observed and learned from the people I would meet, I would gain understanding and knowledge. That belief had served me well in the past. I held no doubts, only dizzying anticipation. At Jennings Creek, years ago, I saw the sun paint the edges of ruffled wet moss with God's presence, now I saw the edges of my life being painted with the same presence, highlighting and deepening all the colors of my every step and turn. How adversity had played its part, was still a mystery. What was not a mystery was that I had been given three unsurpassable gifts: the ability to persevere, deep inner peace and I had been a child of the hills.

EPILOGUE

With my dream of teaching still tightly held, I enrolled at Wayne University in September, 1952.

The previous summer, I worked full time at Parke Davis Pharmaceutical, south of East Jefferson Avenue and earned enough money to pay the $97.50 tuition fee for each of the first two semesters of College. I worked at the Mary Jane Blouse Shop on Woodward Avenue during the coming year to earn spending money. There were many other jobs in the coming four years: giving piano lessons, US. Post Office, D.J. Healy Shops, Grinnell Music Store, Neighborhood Settlement House, and the Kresge Dime Store. Those jobs provided financial need through the remaining three years at Wayne University. My parents provided room and board, at home, during the four years of college.

There were still challenges with transportation during those college years. As in high school, I continued to ride three buses on the Detroit Street Railways (DSR) public transportation system to Wayne University. The end of the third year, I began student teaching assignments at various Detroit Public Schools in a wide range of areas on the city's east and west side, getting there on public transportation was always difficult.

I graduated from Wayne University in August, 1956, although graduates of the August term waited for Commencement Exercises until January, 1957 when the school's name had been changed to Wayne State University. On June 30,1956. I married James Carney. We were married on the week end before the summer semester was completed. Jim, with my parents, attended my Graduation Commencement in January, 1957. My last student teaching assignment in September, 1956, was at the Beech Road Elementary School in Redford Township, Detroit, Michigan. The first six weeks of the semester were unpaid yet part of a year's teaching contract. I held my first kindergarten class in a two room school that used only one of its two rooms. I taught there until January 1958 when I left teaching to have our first child, Brian James. I returned to teaching in 1959 and taught until our second child, Jennifer Colleen was born in 1961. In 1965, six weeks before our third child, John Anthony, was born, we moved to Hemlock, Michigan after having lived in Detroit for twenty-three years. Six weeks later, we moved from Hemlock to Saginaw Township, Michigan where we have lived until the present.

In 1968, I began teaching in the Saginaw Township Community Schools and continued teaching there until 1984. I finished a Master's Degree from the University of Michigan in 1974.

I had a long and rewarding career teaching young children: kindergarten, grades 3, 4 and 5, childcare to high school juniors and seniors and freshmen composition at Great Lakes Community College in Midland, Michigan.

Designed with love by Jennifer Carney
Chicago, 2014